WOMEN
OF THE
JACOBITE
REBELLIONS

WOMEN OF THE JACOBITE REBELLIONS

PHIL CARRADICE

PEN & SWORD HISTORY

AN IMPRINT OF PEN & SWORD BOOKS LTD.
YORKSHIRE – PHILADELPHIA

First published in Great Britain in 2024 by
PEN AND SWORD HISTORY
An imprint of
Pen & Sword Books Ltd
Yorkshire – Philadelphia

Copyright © Phil Carradice, 2024

ISBN 978 1 39905 329 7

The right of Phil Carradice to be identified as Author of this work has been asserted by him in accordance with the Copyright, Designs and Patents Act 1988.

A CIP catalogue record for this book is available from the British Library.

All rights reserved. No part of this book may be reproduced or transmitted in any form or by any means, electronic or mechanical including photocopying, recording or by any information storage and retrieval system, without permission from the Publisher in writing.

Typeset in Times New Roman 11.5/14 by
SJmagic DESIGN SERVICES, India.
Printed and bound in the UK by CPI Group (UK) Ltd.

Pen & Sword Books Limited incorporates the imprints of Atlas, Archaeology, Aviation, Discovery, Family History, Fiction, History, Maritime, Military, Military Classics, Politics, Select, Transport, True Crime, Air World, Frontline Publishing, Leo Cooper, Remember When, Seaforth Publishing, The Praetorian Press, Wharncliffe Local History, Wharncliffe Transport, Wharncliffe True Crime and White Owl.

For a complete list of Pen & Sword titles please contact
PEN & SWORD BOOKS LIMITED
George House, Units 12 & 13, Beevor Street, Off Pontefract Road,
Barnsley, South Yorkshire, S71 1HN, England
E-mail: enquiries@pen-and-sword.co.uk
Website: www.pen-and-sword.co.uk

or

PEN AND SWORD BOOKS
1950 Lawrence Rd, Havertown, PA 19083, USA
E-mail: uspen-and-sword@casematepublishers.com
Website: www.penandswordbooks.com

Contents

Dedication		vi
Introduction		vii
Chapter One	An Introductory Prologue	1
Chapter Two	A Resignation and a Revolution	8
Chapter Three	Mary of Modena and Grizzel Mhor Grant, Jacobite Heroines	17
Chapter Four	Yet More Chances	34
Chapter Five	The '15 Rising: Jacobite Women Flex Their Muscles	43
Chapter Six	Try, Try, Try Again – and an Unexpected Jacobite Heroine	57
Chapter Seven	Jacobite Calling Cards	70
Chapter Eight	The Coming of the Prince and the Lady of Lude	86
Chapter Nine	Culloden and the Women of the Battlefield	95
Chapter Ten	Jacobite Women, Heroes of the '45	110
Chapter Eleven	The Clearances and More	127
Chapter Twelve	Literary Jacobite Women and Men	139
Chapter Thirteen	The End of an Era?	152
Chapter Fourteen	Final Thought	163
Notes		166
Bibliography		171

Dedication

For Grampy and Nanny Carradice – Nanny Donkey as my grandmother was known by everyone in the family – Scotsman and Scotswoman to the bone. When one wasn't regaling me with tales of the '15 and the '45, the other was reading me *Rob Roy* or *Waverley*. Thanks both – this is for you.

My darling Trudy, herself of Scottish descent, and memories of the pair of us trudging around the field of Culloden. It made a change from you hammering the living daylights out of me on the golf course.

Introduction

The Jacobite Risings of the seventeenth and eighteenth centuries – call them invasions, if you like – were far more than military actions in Scotland, England and Ireland. Now, in hindsight, it is easy to say that they were all doomed to fail but without those failures, social development in Britain would have been much slower and more prolonged than they actually were. Put simply, the various risings marked down and contributed to the end of one phase in society and the beginning of another.

The old values and culture, of which James II and his descendants were representatives, was one that was still largely based on feudalism. *The Divine Right of Kings* was the main governing factor of the time and for several hundred years before the first Jacobite rising *social mobility* was virtually unknown, *geographical mobility* only marginally less so.

Where there was a degree of social movement, as seen in the earlier Tudor personalities of men like Cardinal Wolsey and Thomas Cromwell, the adherents to change were looked down upon, even despised by the upper echelons of society. Such attitudes were usually hidden but when they did emerge as in the case of the Duke of Buckingham once pouring wine over Cardinal Wolsey's shoes rather than accept the offered drink – Wolsey never forgot or forgave the insult and, in due time, took his revenge – they provoked bitter responses from both sides of the argument.

The attitude of those with power and money was simple. They were the 'haves', the 'have nots' should be content with their lot. It was a selfish, self-interested viewpoint but one that was considered essential to Stuart philosophy. The idea that people were born into a certain class and position and should therefore exist happily in their natural station in life, without striving to improve those positions, was a point of view that was commonly held.

Had the Jacobites won, had the Stuart dynasty with its adherence to *The Divine Right of Kings* been re-established on the throne, the beginnings of social and even political democracy would have been delayed, maybe even ended before they had really begun. Put simply, the Stuarts and the Jacobites had the romance, the Whig government and the Hanoverian dynasty had the reality!

That does not stop the Jacobite period from being fascinating. However, the romantic and sentimental view of the risings and the history of what had gone on before, as caught in the ballads of the time and in the later works of men like Sir Walter Scott, do tend to overwhelm the reality of the situation.

In many respects, the Hanoverians were actually the good guys, the Jacobites being representatives of an outdated outlaw culture. That, of course, is not how we see them. In fact, most of us take the opposite stance, preferring the romance and the adventure of a hopeless battle to the logical reality of Hanoverian policies for change.

We cheer for Bonnie Prince Charlie hiding and racing through the heather; we condemn Butcher Cumberland for his brutality. To some extent that is understandable. Jesse James and Billy the Kid are our heroes from the American West, not the Pinkertons and men like Sheriff Pat Garrett who hunted down the outlaws and eventually killed them. The seventeenth and eighteenth-century Jacobites fit easily into the same role as the outlaws in the American West.

One of the great failings of the situation concerns the women of the story. Jacobite women remain the unheralded, largely unrecorded heroines of the age. And here, again, there is a comparison to the rugged adventurers of the old West.

Nobody remembers the women, the wives and mothers who drove the covered wagons and accompanied their partners into dangers that nobody could really comprehend. Our attention remains fixed on the range riders, the wagon masters and the scouts, the men with the guns.

Similarly, it is mainly the clansmen and the Rob Roy's of the Jacobite story that we remember; only very rarely do we think of the women. And when we do, they usually appear in the form of a hastily drawn, cliched young girl named Flora MacDonald.

To continue the analogy, without the support and help of those unrecorded American women, the wagon trains would not have reached half way to Tombstone, Deadwood and the rest of the towns in America's

Introduction

Wild West. And so it was with the Jacobite women. Without their help and support the Jacobite cause would have been dead in the water the moment James II left England in 1688. They enabled the clans to rise, created time and space for legends to be born. Regardless of motives, they are an integral part of the Jacobite story.

The history of the Jacobite risings and the role of women within those events is a story well worth telling. They are part of the whole picture and should be considered as such.

So, what do we have? Hopeless and helpless risings doomed to failure? Maybe. The marking of serious social change and development? Quite possibly. Tales of courage and defiance? Most definitely. Read on and find out the truth for yourselves.

Chapter One

An Introductory Prologue

Think about it. For the modern-day writer or historian, perhaps for the historical novelist or simply for any interested party or occasional browser into British history, the Jacobite rebellions and uprisings remain more than a little indefinable. That is a judgement which applies both to Jacobite effectiveness as a political/military entity and, in particular, to the time scale that the period of Jacobinism covered.

To begin with the dreaded rhetorical question, did the Jacobite experience start in 1688 with the Glorious Revolution, a bloodless coup that saw the last Catholic King of England exiled to the continent? Or can its origins be traced back to an earlier date, say to the accession to the English throne of James I, a dour dwarf-like Scotsman with a hide-bound belief in the *Divine Right of Kings*?

Did it end with defeat for Bonnie Prince Charlie on the field of Culloden in April 1746? Or did the outpouring of romantic and sentimentalised love for men who were, effectively, strangers to English, let alone Scottish, traditions and culture, continue apace even after the defeat and routing of the clans. Certainly, that romantic edge made the aftermath and the memory of the various rebellions and risings more dramatic and dangerous than they had ever been in reality.

You could go on interminably, asking more and more unanswerable questions like those. That is a major part of the continuing fascination with the people and the manoeuvrings of the Jacobite era. The doomed efforts to re-establish the rule of King James II, a representative, surely, of the most tragic and unlucky royal family ever to reign in Britain, have left us with a decidedly skewed view of what was really a terrible and troubled time. And that, of course, throws up the most significant argument or discussion point of all.

The continued and continual re-emergence of Jacobite landings or invasions during the late seventeenth and early eighteenth centuries indicates that there must have been some substance to the rebellions other than the romantic cloth of gold that we normally cast over the

Jacobite risings of the time. Doesn't it? The continued drinking of toasts to *The King Over the Water*, long into the nineteenth century and in some quarters at least, would certainly seem to support the notion that Jacobitism did not die in 1746.

Putting aside James II's initial, knee-jerk reaction to losing his throne, something which culminated in an ill-judged invasion of Ireland and defeat at the Battle of the Boyne in 1689, that brings us to the effectiveness of several more significant invasions during the Jacobite period. Again, there emerges the obvious question – were the risings ever a real threat to the late Stuart and early Hanoverian monarchs?

One fact quickly becomes clear. None of the Jacobite gatherings, all of them made up of a great deal more rhetoric than reality, was ever strong enough to raise a serious threat to the Hanoverian monarchy on the island of Great Britain, at least not on their own.

The so-called leaders of the early Jacobite movement, men like the Earl of Mar and Graham of Claverhouse, Bonnie Dundee as he is better known, were undeniably second-raters, aristocrats or minor noblemen who might pose dramatically and talk a good talk about rebellion. Yet they were never strong enough to turn dreams into reality.

As J P Kenyon has observed 'The return of King James always hinged on powerful, outside interventions'.[1] In other words, military, financial and emotional help was required from France, the strongest and most powerful nation in Europe. If France should be unable or unwilling to help, assistance from the Dutch or Spanish was needed. Put simply, no foreign aid, no rebellion.

It was undoubtedly a two-way process. The Jacobite risings offered an opportunity for any or all of Britain's legion of enemies, France in particular, to gain an advantage over her. It was, after all, an age of global warfare with Britain and France usually locked into combat for mastery of Europe and the colonial territories of America.

It was an age of almost continual conflict, from the War of the Spanish Succession to the War of the Quadruple Alliance. Those wars included the wonderfully named War of Jenkins' Ear, a conflict that soon morphed into the more deadly War of the Austrian Succession. Success for the Jacobites in any of these conflicts could produce a crippling blow to British morale, to her economy and to her military strength.[2]

Time and ineffectiveness! They were two vital elements of the Jacobite story that were lacking or unclear. They were both hugely

An Introductory Prologue

important in the eventual defeat of the Old and Young Pretenders, as James III and Charles Edward Stuart were disparagingly known. Perhaps they do contain unanswerable, rhetorical questions but debate about time and effectiveness remain essential elements or components in trying to assess where and why Jacobitism failed.

Ultimately, of course, Jacobitism turned out to be little more than a distant dream, an illusion that was based more on Hanoverian insecurities than on Jacobite strength. That did not stop fear, danger, enthusiasm and a large dose of misjudged patriotism from swelling and covering the land. Quite apart from the serious rebellions and risings, the Jacobite period saw riots in almost every city in Britain. They were the bottom layer in the patriotism and support for the exiled Stuarts. Those riots continued long after Culloden had seemingly ended the Jacobite dream. And in that patriotism, the influence of women cannot be ignored.

The role of women in the Jacobite story has always been something of a side issue, a forgotten enterprise you might say. The image of the Highland warriors rampaging through the Scottish glens and of people like Bonnie Prince Charlie vowing to return and claim his crown have remained the prime images of the Jacobite story. It is perhaps an opportune moment for that to change.

Very little is known about the dreams and activities of the women of the time, particularly those from Scotland. Apart, that is, from Flora MacDonald who has been caught and immortalised for ever as the 'wee Highland lassie', the girl who braved the storm to whisk Charles Edward Stuart 'over the sea to Skye'. So much so that yet another partly rhetorical question immediately springs to mind. Were the female supporters of the Jacobite cause ever there in the first place?

The answer to that is a simple yes; perhaps not for the first attempt by James to reclaim his crown which, technically, was not a Jacobite rising, just an anti-William outburst led by the deposed King James II himself. That took place just four months after his expulsion from England which hardly left time for consideration and proper planning. But they were certainly present at almost every other stage of the coming Jacobite incursions into Hanoverian Britain.

The Jacobite women aided the cause in a wide variety of different ways, from tending wounded soldiers to hiding fugitives who were being pursued by the Hanoverian redcoats, from raising whole regiments of troops to finding money to fund the rebellions. Many of them even ventured out onto the battlefields, before, during and after the action. The women were there, right enough. To think otherwise is to deny the reality of the situation and the times.

And unlike so many of their male companions they continued to be there, to toil and help in whichever way they could, once the final rebellion was finished and the future of Bonnie Prince Charlie's hopes were consigned to the bottom of a whiskey bottle.

Unfortunately, so much of the female help came from what can now only be called anonymous characters, women who rose to the occasion when help was needed and then faded into the background. After all, nobody really remembers a crofters wife or daughter, the shop keeper or the servant girl from the 'big house'. Perform as heroically as they might, women such as that have been melded into the vast array of extras on the Jacobite stage.

And yet, not only were the women present at the gathering of the clans and at the battles, they performed with a gallantry that was at least equal to their men folk. They certainly do not deserve the veil of anonymity that has been drawn across their actions, their personalities and their motivations.

If, as I hope and believe, there is any real purpose behind this book it has to be to tell the Jacobite story. That is, perhaps, a given aim, a logical purpose and design, but, in my mind, I hope to tell it, in part at least, through the eyes of the women who have been ignored for so long.

If it is going to be accurate, no history of the risings can focus on just the women alone. That would be to fall into the same pit of emptiness that engulfed Jenny Cameron, Grizzel Mhor and many others. Just like the male-dominated view of events that we have been presented with over the years it would not show the whole picture of blasted dreams and shattered aims.

What I hope comes across is the story of the Jacobite women combined and entwined with the men who gathered alongside them beneath the flags of the two Pretenders and, initially, of King James II himself. That, I believe, is the only way to tell the full story.

It is not easy to work out why neglect of the part played by Jacobite women should have occurred. It remains one of the great tragedies of the risings when, sadly, the efforts of the women were barely recognised, not even by the major figures of the time. Or, for that matter, by the press. Where those efforts were occasionally appreciated, they were still tinged with irony and anger. The attitude of Charles Stuart is a classic example.

An Introductory Prologue

Charles Edward Stuart, the Young Pretender, Bonnie Prince Charlie, the Young Chevalier – call him what you will – might have appreciated Flora MacDonald's courage and stamina but he bitterly resented her sharp tongue and the rebukes she gave him for his 'regal ways and manners' when he was supposed to be acting as her servant. Put simply, nobody had ever spoken to him like that before.

When his flight was over, Charles and Flora went their separate ways, as might be expected of two people from such different social classes. The romantic idea of a distant love between the two is no more than a piece of fictional nonsense and owes its origins and continued acceptance to *The Skye Boat Song* and other sentimental ballads.

The women of Scotland sacrificed so much, not just during the campaigns but also in the Highland Clearances which followed the final rising. For those who understood what was happening and why, it was a heart-breaking involvement:

> Soldiers of a desperate cause, these mothers, wives and daughters showed not only courage in hours of acute danger, but the resolute spirit of self-sacrifice that never shrunk under a life-time of adversity and of broken fortunes.[3]

In the glens and bothies of Scotland's traditional male-orientated society, that spirit of self-sacrifice was almost unheard of, let alone encountered. In that respect, Jacobitism was truly a revolutionary movement.

No matter who they were or whatever their role in life, for many of the women, the Jacobite risings were an emotional, almost hysterical, response to what can now be seen as a tyrannical exercise in central government.

Most of them would hardly have been able to express it as such but support for the Old and Young Pretenders and for the Jacobite cause, in general, was a revolutionary addition to already existing anti-royalist ideology. The fact that the Jacobite cause was firmly based in support of the old regal regime, symbolised by James, by his son and by his grandson, was conveniently ignored.

Jacobitism was, at the end of the day, a kick against the growth of a more democratic society as represented by the new Hanoverian rulers. Despite the growth and importance of overseas trade, the Hanoverian version of capitalism was resented by many and manifested itself, with both men and women in Britain, as a unique revolutionary spirit that has ramifications even today.[4]

The name Jacobite was derived from the word Jacobus, Latin for James. It was used initially in a derogatory way, symbolising those who fought against, first, the supporters of the new monarchs, King William III and Queen Mary II and then, once George I became King, against the Hanoverians. Parliament and those who had invited William and Mary to come and take the crown should have realised that the situation was perfectly set up for conflict.

The likelihood of war and revolution was where the fervent Nationalism that is still inherent in the memory of the risings first came to be apparent, particularly in Scotland and Ireland. That Nationalism has never gone away in either of the two largest Celtic countries, even though the rebellious nature of Jacobitism soon took on a somewhat different guise for the Irish following defeat at the Battle of the Boyne.

In Ireland, following what many considered their abandonment by James II, the Jacobites came to worry less about the restoration of James Stuart and more about creating an independent, free-standing Ireland. That was something which James had opposed when he was king and there is no doubt that if he had been returned to his throne troubles of a different sort would have emerged.

Also quite different, the Jacobites of Wales – the last of the 'four nations' to make up the British Isles – adopted yet another approach. Despite being just as Celtic in their roots, the Welsh were far less violent in their approach.

Wales had been legally united with England since Henry VIII's Acts of Union in the 1530s, nearly 200 years before the eruption of Jacobite rebellion and risings. And that had undoubtedly affected the attitude of the Welsh people who were happy to express support but were not so inclined to take up arms on behalf of the Jacobites and their Catholic religion.

Another factor to be considered is that by the time of the two main insurrections, the '15 and the '45 as they are known, the priority goal for most Scottish Jacobites was not the return of their Catholic King but the ending of the 1707 Union between Scotland and England.

The Scottish Act of Union had been hurriedly pushed through Parliament. Approved by Anne – who was then Queen, the last of the Stuart monarchs – it dissolved the Scottish Parliament and effectively joined the two countries together as one united nation.

An Introductory Prologue

Passing the Act of Union was a high-handed action, designed to create the situation which the ruling body considered appropriate for its subjects, a classic example of the tyrannical behaviour so hated by the rebellious few.

No one had considered Scottish opinion on the matter or if they did it was simply ignored. While hugely evocative and distressing for the Scots, the Act of Union had little or no relevance for Wales or, for that matter, for Ireland either.

While there was considerable Welsh support for the various risings, that support consisted mainly of cryptic toasts and muffled debate in drinking societies like *The Sea Sergeants of South Wales*. Support in North Wales was a little stronger where *The Cycle of the White Rose* was led by Sir Watkin Williams-Wynn, one of the most important landowners of the region.

At various times a number of Welsh zealots did march off to join the various Jacobite armies and Gwent lawyer David Morgan from the *Sea Sergeants* even managed to get himself hanged for treason. But there was no sudden rising of Welsh Jacobites, leaving historians and writers with the idea that the Welsh Jacobites could talk a good talk but that was where their opposition to the Hanoverian government began and ended.

While several of the potentially militant and more dangerous Welsh supporters of the exiled King were arrested before they could undertake any type of military action, it is probable that even without that 'police state' intervention, very little more violence would have occurred in the Principality. As far as Wales was concerned, the Jacobite cause and the events that accompanied it were little more than a damp squib.

There remains a lighter side to the affair, however, when the most notable aspect of Welsh support came in a comment made by Bonnie Prince Charlie after the failure of the last rising. He glibly commented 'I will do for the Welsh Jacobites what they did for me. I will drink their health.'[5]

The Jacobite risings were the final lurch in the Stuart desire to regain power and control in Britain. Destined never to succeed, the rebellions have left us with a romantic story that has warmed many a heart and made the winter nights around the fireside somewhat more bearable. That is perhaps its greatest achievement.

The Jacobite rebellions are, in the main, the stuff of fantasy. They are as relevant as the efforts of JRR Tolkien or the creators of *The Game of Thrones*. But like those fictional efforts, they remain fascinating, enthralling even, in their ability to provide us with interest and comfort. And perhaps it is now time for the role of the Jacobite women to be added to those comforts.

Chapter Two

A Resignation and a Revolution

As Charles Dickens once said 'Tell them what you're going to tell them, tell them, then tell them what you just told them.' Following that precept, this, in a nutshell, is the story of how the Jacobite risings began:

James I of England (James VI of Scotland) had come to the throne of England in 1603, in the wake of a most glorious period of plenty, when the country had been ruled over by possibly the greatest dynasty in English history. The Tudors, either by accident or by design, had managed to create a magnificent edifice of culture and martial power that were the envy and, in many respects, the terror of the known world.

Queen Elizabeth, James' immediate predecessor, was the most splendid and, in hindsight, the most successful of them all. In drama and poetry, in fashion and design, in architecture and painting, the reign produced work of rare quality. Militarily it was a similar success; England had defeated the might of Spain and now English privateers roamed unchecked across the seas. It was not for nothing that the period has gone down in history as the years of Elizabethan glory and fame.

And yet, no matter how glorious – perhaps showy might be a better description – Elizabeth's period in power might have been, it had failed to address so many issues. All too often the Queen and her advisors only glossed over a legion of significant problems that were soon to beset the country.

To begin with there were the religious differences and issues that had plagued England during the reigns of Henry VIII, Edward VI and Mary and then stumbled on to trouble Elizabeth. The fact that many of those differences had been self-inflicted by the Tudors did not, in any way, ease their effect on the nation.

Then there was a vast stockpile of social problems which showed that Elizabeth had not given anything more than lip service towards alleviating the difficulties that were gathering momentum in the towns and countryside. Beggars and vagrants roamed the hills and roads, enclosures had caused widespread poverty and displacement. Discontent was gathering like a distant thunder storm.

The economic tensions and the rise of the middle classes, still relatively powerless and unrepresented but already bitterly resentful, were another linked pair of issues. They had been all-too-easily glossed over and hidden by Elizabeth's various governments.

Elizabeth, because of her power, because of her reputation, because of her ability to handle people, had been able to 'keep the lid' on what was a simmering pot of anger. The new King James, a small but belligerent Scot whose accent was so thick he had difficulty making himself understood, had neither her ability nor her charm so that he and his son, the future Charles I, inherited what was an explosive combination of discontent and impending danger. Disaster would inevitably come. It was just a case of finding out when that was likely to happen.

If the reign of King James was to prove a difficult and troubled one, then Charles I's period in power was nothing short of chaos. Dispute with Parliament centred inevitably on the traditional Stuart belief in the Divine Right of Kings, saw Civil War, the death in combat of thousands and the eventual execution of the monarch. Oliver Cromwell and the Commonwealth brought a degree of stability and were finally succeeded by the restoration of the monarchy. In 1660 the delayed arrival of a new king saw Charles II on the throne. And that is where our swift sweep or retrospective of sixty years of British history ends, and the Jacobite story really begins.

The British people were more than happy to see Charles II crowned as king, even to accept his religious leanings towards Papal acceptance and control. Rumour later came to declare that Charles had converted to Catholicism on his deathbed but in 1660 such ideas were beyond countenance.

The new King's religious beliefs were, after all, leanings not a stated position and the rigours of Puritanism, which had been settled on the country after the killing of King Charles I had begun to pall for most people. Oliver Cromwell had been strong enough to sustain the Puritan ideal, his son Richard Cromwell, Tumbledown Dick as he soon became known, was not.

England, in the shape of Parliament, was also content to acknowledge the position of Charles' brother James as his successor. The two brothers had been estranged but by the time of the Restoration they had reconciled their differences and the line of succession had been established. As long as Charles had no heir that was how it would be, despite James' conversion to Catholicism in 1668. That religious change had been kept secret but, like all matters of state and royalty, news of James' conversion soon leaked out.

In light of that conversion, continued acceptance of James as heir to the throne was a risk. But it was one that the staunchly Protestant English were willing to take. The alternative was a return to the chaos of the Civil War and its aftermath. The way Parliament looked at it, one Catholic king – in this case James – was acceptable, a whole dynasty of them was not. And that meant the successor to James, whoever that might be, would have to be carefully chosen, his or her position managed with care and understanding.

The twenty-plus years of Charles' reign were far from easy. Difficulties manifested themselves in a series of wars with the Dutch, a brutal visitation of the plague and, above all, continual discord between Protestants and Catholics. The tension was fuelled by people like Titus Oates and his fiendish but imaginary Popish Plot which centred on a devious and non-existent Catholic plan to assassinate and then replace the King and his brother.

Relationships between England and Scotland were not good, either. Economic and religious difficulties meant that the homeland of the Stuart dynasty was undoubtedly 'the poor relation' in the disparate family of Britain. Even after the rejection of James and the instillation of the Hanoverians things failed to improve:

> The crises of the 1690s had impoverished the nation while in the short run, the 1707 union with England did little to improve the economy. Scotland remained one of the poorest countries in Europe.[1]

Further argument between members of Parliament – a Protestant body, if ever there was one – and the country's minority core of Catholics simply added to the concerns. Anti-Catholic riots were not exactly common but in 1677, just prior to Titus Oates' Popish Plot, they reached new heights. It was a time of great concern and worry. If one person managed to keep the peace it was Charles II and, at least to begin with, he did it rather well.

In the early days of the reign, both Charles and James were relatively popular figures. They had gone into exile while Oliver Cromwell's Commonwealth had been in place and, in the minds of many, represented a happy and glorious time gone by. They were also brave and capable soldiers, exactly the attributes the English wanted from their rulers.

James, in particular, had performed with courage and dignity in the service of his cousin, Louis XIV of France, fighting furiously in conflicts against the Fronde and opposing those countries involved in the Spanish Alliance. The Battle of the Dunes in 1658 had presented him with the perfect opportunity to display his reckless courage.

When Oliver Cromwell signed a peace accord with the French, James was forced to leave France. He switched his allegiance (and his location or base) to Spain where he came increasingly under the influence of the Catholic church. It was a significant moment for the young man.

After the Restoration of 1660 and once established again in England, James was recognised as the Duke of York and was appointed Lord High Admiral. This meant him taking control of the Royal Navy during three Anglo-Dutch Wars. He saw action in the Americas and off the coast of Africa where he was instrumental in gaining English control of the lucrative slave trade.

It was the Great Fire of London in 1666, however, that really established James as a popular favourite with the London populace. When the fire broke out on Sunday 2 September, the King passed to his brother control of the efforts to check the blaze. Using the Trained Bands and volunteer firemen James promptly set up and took command of over fifty makeshift firefighting bases across London.

For three full days, he was a constant presence at these bases, urging continued effort and directing the fire-fighting operations. These operations ranged from pulling down houses in order to create fire breaks to directing buckets and sprays of water at the flames. But no matter how diligently he performed his job it was a hopeless task. Samuel Pepys, present throughout the fire, wrote about James' actions:

> There was little that could be done, the fire coming upon them so fast - - -he (the Duke of York) commanded the Lord Mayor to spare no houses but to pull them down before the fire. The Duke of York bid me to tell him that if he would have any more soldiers, he would have them.[2]

The problem was really the narrow streets, lined by scores of churches, warehouses and old wooden houses. Once the fire took hold it spread rapidly, more rapidly than any man could predict. In the end, before the fire was extinguished, approximately 13,000 houses and nearly a hundred churches were destroyed. Partly due to the work of James and his fire fighters, only four lives were lost.

The efforts of James, to put out the fire and yet preserve as many houses as possible, might have been a fruitless exercise but they did not go unnoticed by Londoners:

> The Duke of York hath won the hearts of the people with his continual and indefatigable pains, day and night, in helping to quell the fire.[3]

It was the highpoint of James' time as heir apparent to the throne. From there he could only ever go in one direction – downwards.

* * *

The last portion of Charles' reign was one of considerable apprehension, not to say outright fear. As the death of the monarch approached the prospect of a coming Catholic King did not lie easily on the minds and hearts of a staunchly Protestant people. But James was already the chosen man and had been for years. For most of the English population, the one consolation was that after his death, the crown would pass to his daughter Mary, a confirmed Protestant married to William of Orange, the religious leader of Protestant Europe.

Long term, therefore, people consoled themselves with the thought that everything would be all right, it would all work out. It was the immediate that was the main worry. And that was a real concern. Whatever the distant future might hold, twenty or thirty years of Catholic rule under James could easily bring all sorts of damage to the Protestant religion. And Mary's succession was not guaranteed. Everything hinged on James not having children and on his Protestant daughter succeeding, untroubled, to the English throne.

James and his wife Anne Hyde were unfortunate in that six of their children had died young, leaving only Mary and her sister Anne to continue the line. That, of course, suited the English Parliament and when Anne Hyde died in 1671, the members gave a collective sigh of relief. No wife meant no legitimate children. And in the case of James, that meant no Catholic successor.

In 1673 James spoiled the scenario by marrying again, this time to the Italian and staunchly Catholic Mary of Modena. To begin with, the second marriage of James seemed to be proceeding in a similar fashion to his first, the new Queen being afflicted by a series of miscarriages and still births. It seemed to be almost a tradition for the future King to see his offspring wither and die in front of his eyes. Inevitably, many Protestant zealots believed it was the will of God.

The Exclusion Crisis of 1679 was the result of a proposal by the Earl of Shaftesbury, a move which could possibly debar James from the succession. The proposal was eventually defeated but not before Parliament had divided itself into two distinct parties, the Whigs who supported Shaftesbury's motion and the Tories who opposed it. The two groups, soon to become Britain's first political parties, would play significant roles in the various stages of the coming Jacobite rebellions.

Charles II died in February 1685 and James duly succeeded to the throne. As might be expected, relationships between the new King and his Protestant subjects were not good. But with Parliament, in the wake of the Exclusion Crisis, they were particularly tense. When, in 1687 James devised the Declaration of Indulgence and announced that he was in favour of freedom of worship for everyone, including Catholics, it simply confirmed the worst fears of the rabidly biased and bigoted Protestant majority.

The appointment of Catholic officers to significant positions in the army, Catholicising as it became known, was yet another annoyance to the Protestants. Soon almost every significant army post was occupied by a Catholic. When, in 1687, James disbanded Parliament with a view to reassembling it as he saw fit, it was clear that the King was trying to create a representative body that would provide him with unconditional support. The Declaration of Indulgence, which suspended all anti-Catholic laws, simply added to the troubles. Shades of Charles I and the run-up to the Civil War seemed to be hovering over everything James either did or thought.

As if all that was not enough, disaster was waiting in the wings, a seventeenth-century 'spanner in the works'. In 1688 the news that Mary of Modena had given birth to a healthy baby boy came like a thunderbolt to the people of England. King James immediately had him christened James Francis Edward and given the traditional title of Prince of Wales. James was just as quick to announce that the child would be brought up as a Catholic.

The rumour spread that Mary had not given birth at all. There *was* a child, the gossip mongers said, but he was 'bought in' and brought from the backstreets of London, smuggled into the birthing chamber in a warming pan. The story was ridiculous but was proof that the pro-Protestant/anti-James lobby had grown frantic in the attempt to keep a Catholic prince from succeeding to the throne after the present king.

The same year as the birth of the new Prince of Wales saw the prosecution of a number of Puritans, charged with seditious libel. In July 1688 they were acquitted but the affair damaged James' political standing. It led to the next dramatic step in the King's downfall and after that, events unravelled quickly.

Seven Protestant peers now took the drastic step of writing to Duke William in the Netherlands, pledging him their support should he ever decide to invade England. William of Orange, whose wife had just lost her role as successor to the English crown, had actually been exploring that possibility, even going so far as to gather together extra troops under his command – just in case.

James was no mean soldier, and a ruthless one at that. He had already dealt with the organisers of what was known as the Rye House Plot, a flawed and unlikely attempt to kill him and his brother Charles and replace them with William of Orange.

Since becoming King, James had also taken to the field to defeat the Duke of Monmouth, the illegitimate son of Charles II, at the Battle of Sedgemoor. The Duke was outnumbered and quickly captured before being taken to London where he was executed. The Battle of Sedgemoor saw the emergence of a new and highly efficient general, John Churchill, who as the Duke of Marlborough would go on to greater things in the reign of the Queen Anne.

More significantly, Sedgemoor was the last time an English monarch would lead his troops into battle on English soil and James followed up his victory by unleashing Judge George Jeffreys in a cruel and brutal act of revenge. Over 250 rebels were executed, many more transported in what became known as the Bloody Assizes, thanks to the hanging judge. It was a barbaric response to a pointless rebellion and it was not forgotten by the supporters of William of Orange.

In November 1688, news reached James that his son-in-law had climbed down from the fence and taken the fatal step of landing with an army of 15,000 men at Torbay in Devon. The King immediately gathered his own forces and set out to confront the invaders.

Unfortunately, James was unwell, suffering from a downturn in health that was to plague him for the rest of his life. Emotionally he was in equally as bad a state and when several important members of his staff, including relatives and significant figures like John Churchill began to desert in order to join William, the King quickly became distraught.

He turned his army around and headed back to London. From there he announced that he was willing to accept a 'free Parliament' rather than a purely advisory body called and dismissed on the whim of the monarch. In reality, however, James was already making plans to leave the country. What followed was nothing less than a grand farce.

In December 1688 James and his family attempted to leave England. Having paused to throw the Great Seal of State into the Thames, the royal party set out for Kent with a view to taking a ship for France. They failed to get very far before they were caught and brought back to London.

A second escape attempt later in the month was more successful. William of Orange had no desire to create a royal martyr and surreptitiously arranged or oversaw the escape of his father-in-law. Mary of Modena apparently escaped London dressed as a laundress. James did not mind how he and his family were going to leave – as long as they could get away he was content. There were more conducive countries in Europe.

Free of the country that he had now grown to dislike, even hate, James took up residence in France where his cousin Louis XIV, known to posterity as the Sun King, was on the throne. Gradually more and more supporters of the displaced King began to join him so that when he died in 1701 James was at the centre of a significant exile court.

Back in Britain, James' supposed loyal servants quickly began to rearrange the structure of their society. They met in what was known as the Convention Parliament and at the end of December 1688, under a fair degree of pressure from William, agreed to a joint monarchy. Mary would be Queen, William the King.

In Scotland, the Convention of Estates also met to discuss the succession. Debate was long and hard, their decision finally being made in May 1689. Letters from James and William presented to the Scottish Convention for debate and discussion had revealed his uncompromising position with regard to religion and his powers or rights as king. It was something that undoubtedly played a part in their final decision:

> He even threatened those who might not be willing to submit to his rule. In effect, by this approach, the last Stuart king committed political suicide. The Convention's decision to invite William and Mary to accept the crown of Scotland was, therefore, almost a foregone conclusion.[4]

The Scottish Convention, clear now that James had literally forfeited his crown, passed their resolution with only four opposing votes.[5]

The Declaration of Right, passed by the English Parliament that same year, placed many restrictions on royal authority, restrictions with which William and Mary had no power or real inclination to disagree or deny. Chief amongst them was the right to call and retain regular Parliaments without approval of the sovereign but there was also the clause that no Catholic would ever again become the English monarch.

The Glorious Revolution was hardly a coup, James being more than happy to escape with his life. He was unwell and possibly not thinking clearly but it was obvious to everyone that he valued his religion far more than he did his crown.

The term Glorious Revolution was not in common use at the time but was later adopted by the Protestants, John Hamden first coining the phrase in 1689. For the Whigs in Parliament and in the country the affair became known as The Bloodless Revolution while the Catholic minority termed it simply as The Revolution of 1688.

Whatever it was called there was surprisingly little opposition to the desertion of James II. Some small risings or murmurs of discontent took place in Scotland and Ireland, none at all in England or Wales. Where risings or riots did occur, they were quickly subdued. A few similar uprisings occurred in the American Colonies but what little disagreement there was from the lands across the sea also soon disintegrated.

The general consensus was that James had not been defeated or deposed. He had simply vacated his throne and therefore the country was well rid of him.

There was still some way to go but the accession of William and Mary was the beginning of true democracy in Britain and from that moment on the whole concept of sovereignty changed. It became something derived, gifted or given, by Parliament – in other words – the people. No longer was the succession simply a matter of accident of birth or, as in so many cases of the past, by sheer military might. Now it was, in theory at least, a matter of meritocracy.

Chapter Three

Mary of Modena and Grizzel Mhor Grant, Jacobite Heroines

The Bloodless or Glorious Revolution of 1688 witnessed the physical and political disappearance from Britain of James, his whole family and entourage. And that included the woman who, by the sheer gynaecological accident of being in the wrong place at the wrong time, had begun the whole problem of succession and the subsequent flight of the King – Mary of Modena.

Already a titled Princess from the Duchy of Modena in North-West Italy, Mary's marriage to James had been an arranged one. They were married by proxy on 30 September 1673, without ever having seen each other. Pausing briefly at King Louis's new palace of Versailles, where she charmed the French King and his court with her beauty and behaviour, Mary then journeyed to London to meet her husband for the first time.

At first sight, Mary was not impressed either by James' appearance or by his demeanour. She was particularly upset by his face – scarred from smallpox – and by his typical Stuart stutter which made communication between the two newlyweds rather difficult. For some time, she apparently dissolved into tears whenever she saw him. However, Mary eventually came to love both her husband and the son, James Francis Edward (the Old Pretender), that she had borne him.

Mary and James were to have just one more surviving child, duly christened Louisa Maria Teresa, a young girl who was not involved in the Jacobite wars and invasions. She was to die from smallpox shortly before Mary's own demise some years later.

Mary developed a good relationship with her namesake, the Princess Mary, daughter of James and his first wife Anne Hyde, even travelling to the Netherlands to see her once she was married to William of Orange. Anne, the other surviving daughter from James' previous marriage, did not like her new stepmother and, despite repeated attempts at compromise and offers of friendship from Mary, kept a wary distance.

Mary of Modena had no interest in politics. Her concerns were for her family and for the lives that she saw played out before them. She was a well-educated woman who spoke Italian, French and Latin and soon grasped the intricacies of the English language. Possessed of a ready wit, she gave James a degree of approachability that he had never had before.

Mary was not popular with the Protestant English, however. They called her 'The Pope's Daughter', a term derived more from her staunch Catholic beliefs and the personality of her husband than from any deficiencies of her own. Her Catholicism aggravated Protestant sensibilities, over-rode her qualities and pushed James further to the extremities of English social life.

At one stage the English Parliament even threatened to have the marriage of James and Mary annulled, although how likely or valid such a step would have been remains unknown. Likely or not, the threat to his brother's marriage forced Charles, then the English king, to suspend Parliament for several months and the popularity of the royal family took a sharp decline.

Yet, despite what might initially seem to be a recipe for disaster, Mary and James managed to survive the crisis, thanks in the main to the charm and personality of the Italian Princess.

She might have had a limited range of concerns or outlooks on the religious and political problems of the Stuart dynasty but the new Queen soon won over the senior members of her husband's entourage. It was a small chink that did not even make a mark with the more rabid opponents of the King but it was a start. To the more volatile of his supporters, after accompanying James into exile in 1688 Mary became known fondly as 'The Queen Over the Water'

Both in that title and by her later actions while in exile on the Continent, Mary of Modena became a significant figure in early Jacobite circles. So significant, in fact, that arguably she deserves to be given the epithet of the 'First of the Jacobite Women'.

Distanced by rank and position from the majority of the Jacobite supporters, to the end of her life Mary still managed to provide emotional and financial aid to many of those who had accompanied the royal family into exile. That was something James signally failed to do.

Acknowledged by Louis XIV as the true king and queen of England, Scotland and Ireland, James II along with Mary and their son took up residence in the Chateau de Saint-Germain-en-Laye, the old French palace. It was no great hardship for Louis as Versailles, the new palace he had commissioned and built, had now grown into one of the most opulent royal houses in Europe. James and Mary furnished their own palace in some style, perhaps not as notable as that of the Sun King, but more than comfortable for a royal dynasty in exile.

They quickly became popular members of the French establishment – or at least Mary did. She was charming and witty, full of good humour and fun and became a leading member of Louis' court. James, on the other hand, was regarded as a bore. As one French wit declared 'When James spoke you understood why he had lost his crown.'[1]

Despite her lack of interest in politics, Mary supported her husband in all of his attempts to win back the English crown. Not unduly rich or self-sufficient, she still knew where her duty lay. She bought, provisioned and despatched three supply ships to Bantry Bay to assist James in his 1689 invasion of Ireland. She also donated £2000 to the rebel Jacobite army that was then gathering in Dunbar, funding the gift by selling almost all of her jewellery.

Mary remained unstinting in her efforts to help James' friends and supporters. She was well aware of her own privileged position which, even in exile, stood in contrast to the poverty that afflicted many of the exiled Jacobites in France. She gave generously to them whenever she was asked and often before any request came her way. She even encouraged her children to donate what they could out of their 'pocket money' – an interesting concept, given the time and the situation.

He had been in poor health for several years but, finally King James II died of a seizure on 16 September 1701. He had already been partially paralysed by a stroke some months earlier. The young James Francis Edward Stuart was immediately proclaimed King James III – by everyone, it seemed, apart from the English Parliament – and promised all sorts of support from his uncle Louis.

However, as he was only thirteen years old, James was too young to assume the nominal reins of government with the result that Mary of Modena became Regent. By the terms of the Regency agreement, she agreed to support and guide her son until he reached the age of sixteen.

Politics and diplomacy might have been uncongenial to her but Mary applied herself to her task with a skill and efficiency that so many Jacobites seemed to lack. She was helped by her innate wisdom and intelligence and by her caring, compassionate nature.

Even though Mary and her family were in exile there was still much to be done if they wished to continue with their aim of being reinstated to the English throne. Mary was soon presiding over her son's Regency Council and supervising the printing and production of a Manifesto outlining the claims of the young James. It was largely ignored in England and Scotland, but it was a necessary document in establishing the credibility of the Jacobite claims.

Twelve years after the death of James II the War of the Spanish Succession, which had been raging for some time, was finally drawn to a close in 1713 by the signing of the Treaty of Utrecht. By the terms of this Treaty and by the Anglo-French Alliance of 1712, the Jacobites were obliged to withdraw their presence from France. Most of them found other homes for themselves in the Low Countries or Italy. But not Mary.

For 'The Queen Over the Water', Saint-Germaine had been her home since 1688. There was no way she was going to lose it now. And so, she stayed. With her son rapidly approaching his majority her work was almost done and so she remained in a non-political position at her home in Paris nursing her dying daughter and attending to her own ill health.

It was probably something of a relief for Mary. In the final years of her Regency, she had hosted a number of politicians and statesmen from Britain, many of them charlatans, others eager to find a solution to the Jacobite problem. Separating the good from the bad, the genuine from the fakes, had required huge tact and skill on Mary's part.

Notable amongst these visitors and diplomats was Lord Belhaven who came to Paris with an intricate plan to place the young James on the throne. James would need to undertake a conversion to Protestantism, Belhaven declared, but, in return, he would be guaranteed a number of Catholic Bishops in the Anglican Church.

A visit by Lord Lovat took place on the death of King William III in 1702. A renowned wheeler and dealer who changed sides whenever the whim took him, Lovat arrived in an effort to end the stalemate and made offers similar to those of Lord Belhaven. During Mary's Regency, there were several other 'diplomatic' missions, most of them hinging on the requirement of James converting to the Catholic faith. Mary turned them all down.

The reason for her repeated rejections was simple enough. Each plan would have needed the young James to take up residence in Scotland or England. Mary, only too well aware of the duplicity of the English and Scottish nobles, was never going to expose her son to dangers like the ones he would face back in Great Britain.

Mary of Modena died from breast cancer in 1718. It was a protracted and painful end but she saw it through with the indomitable courage that she had displayed throughout her life. A remarkable woman, she truly deserves the title of the First Jacobite Woman – first in the number of female Jacobite supporters who rallied to James' side and, perhaps more significantly, first in the importance of her support for the Jacobite cause.

* * *

At the risk of confusing readers, in order to make the story complete we need to briefly go back to 1689, the first year of exile for James II. His departure from England had been rapid but within a few months, sitting in the security of Chateau de Saint-Germain-en-Laye, he began to have doubts about the wisdom of his actions. Louis, who had been waging war against Williamite England for some time, had promised military help in any attempt James might make in an effort to regain his throne and the exiled King began to rekindle his courage.

His flight in 1688 had been an ignominious way to leave the throne. When mixed with what, in hindsight, had been a terrible blow to James' pride, along with the ever-present Stuart belief in the Divine Right of Kings, a whole mix of emotions persuaded the fugitive King to attempt to push back the clock. It was time to regain his power and position.

James looked, first, to Ireland. The Irish Parliament had not followed the example of England and Scotland. They had claimed that James was still king and passed a Bill of Attainder against anyone who opposed him. To James, it therefore seemed as if Ireland was a good place to start. His plan was simple. He would first defeat William's armies in Ireland and then use the country as a stronghold and a springboard from which he could attack and make inroads into England.

Mary of Modena had grave doubts about the enterprise. Her husband, she knew, was far from fit and well and she was afraid of what might happen in Ireland. She had already begun to enjoy her time in France, finding it far more congenial than the cold and unwelcoming British Isles. Yet she knew her duty and gave her support, emotional and practical, to her husband. As James paraded and played at soldiery, Mary was already making plans to send him extra supplies, money and troops.

Meanwhile, James gathered together his forces, most of them French soldiers offered or donated by his cousin Louis, and prepared to invade. He had approximately 30 ships under his command and landed in Kinsale on 14 March 1689. There, he was immediately joined by large numbers of Irish Jacobites. The Irish had already been fighting the English forces of William, the Williamites as they were termed, part of the on-going war against France and they were battle-hardened and ready to defend the rights of the man they still saw as their King.

James concentrated his forces in two main areas, in the south behind the line of the River Shannon and, in the largely Protestant north, around the strategically important town of Derry. After a brief foray northwards, a journey that involved him entering Dublin to call the Irish Parliament, James remained with the southern group while a number of his senior generals gathered their forces outside Derry. Eventually, the Jacobites in the north numbered approximately 12,000 men.

The Protestant enclave of Derry had already come under attack in December of the previous year, soon after the news of the King's flight became public knowledge. Jacobite forces nearly made it through the town gates but a band of thirteen Derry apprentices raced to the entrance and slammed the doors shut. The Jacobites went away, mortified and defeated. Now it was time to try again.

The siege of Derry began on 18 April 1689 and dragged on for 105 days. The high point, or the low one, depending on how you view it, came when Jacobite General Conrad von Rosen gathered together dozens of women and children from the surrounding countryside and forced them to huddle alongside the town walls. In that exposed position they were certain to become casualties. The Williamites inside the town retaliated by threatening to kill their prisoners and Rosen was forced to withdraw the women.

Conditions in the besieged town were horrendous, hundreds dying from the starvation and sickness that afflicted most besieged towns.

Eventually, however, a relief fleet managed to make it through the Jacobite blockade and ease the suffering of the people in the town.

Faced by a relieved garrison, Conrad von Rosen decided that enough was enough. On 1 August he drew back his forces and ended the siege. It had cost somewhere in the region of 4000 to 6000 deaths, most of them innocent civilians from inside Derry. Women, perhaps inevitably, suffered the worst, trying to keep their families fed and helping out in the defence of the town walls.

Defeat at the Battle of Newtownbutler, not long after the siege of Derry was lifted, added to James' woes. It was clear that he had lost control of the north, a situation which did not seem likely to change, and Ulster and the rest of the region remained firmly pro-monarchy and Protestant.

In the south, it seemed at first as if things might play out differently. The Williamite army in the region, under the command of Friedrich Hermann Von Schonberg, was short on supplies and ravaged by sickness. Taking advantage of this, James managed to capture Carrickfergus and set up a camp north of Dundalk. However, he held off attacking the main Williamite force, a delay that was to cost him dearly.

King William saw the danger and immediately brought reinforcements, fresh troops and supplies, from England. He was now present in Ireland for any future battle, just as James was there with the Jacobites. In the end, William's 30,000 soldiers significantly outnumbered the Jacobites who were now also suffering from sickness.

The Battle of the Boyne was fought on 1 July 1689. It was a bloody affair that saw 1500 Jacobites and 800 Williamites killed in the combat and many more, from both sides, severely wounded. King William was himself hit in the shoulder by a ricochet bullet. He was lucky, it was a flesh wound, but his general Friedrich Hermann Von Schonberg was not so fortunate. He was killed in the closing stages of the battle.

Victory finally went to William. Seeing that the game was up, James felt he had no alternative but to escape. He headed for the coast, took ship and returned to France. He may well have been taking the logical political move but his disappearance did not sit easily with the members of his entourage, particularly as he was never again to set foot in Ireland.

James' defection – or desertion as they saw it – was soundly cursed by his Jacobite supporters, many of whom promptly gave up on the cause and returned to their homes. Some fought on, supported by French arms and men. Defeat at Aughrim came in July and in October Limerick surrendered to the Williamite forces. Offered generous terms, most of the French soldiers in the garrison were sent back to their homeland.

Jacobitism in Ireland was far from dead, however. Large numbers still fought on but even in their disgust they bestowed on the exiled king the name 'Seamus an Claca', in other words 'James the Shit'.

* * *

James' ill-fated invasion of Ireland had been a disaster, a case of opportunities presented to the Jacobites and then quickly lost. And the missed opportunities continued to abound. In 1690 an Anglo-Dutch fleet was soundly defeated by the French off Beachy Head. It meant that, for a while at least, all of England's south coast was open to invasion but, once again, the advantage was not pressed home and the English navy soon recovered control of the Channel.[2]

James' landing in Ireland was accompanied by a significant rising in Scotland. The two events were hardly co-ordinated, another example of a lost opportunity. Individual enterprise could only ever go so far, a lesson that James and his advisors failed to grasp.

The Scottish rebellion was led by John Graham, Viscount of Dundee, a popular figure in Scotland. He was a handsome man, imbued with many of the traits that later came to symbolize Jacobite leaders and was better known as Bonnie Dundee. He was not, however, a particularly clever general.

The Scottish Jacobites rose soon after James landed in Ireland, most of Dundee's army being comprised of clansmen and Highlanders. Support for the rising was limited – perhaps if James had been present things might have been different but he was too preoccupied with his Irish adventure. Even so, there was initial success for the Jacobites.

At Killiecrankie on 27 July 1689 John Graham was confronted by a Williamite army under General Hugh Mackay. At first glance, it appeared as if the Jacobite cause was hopeless but Bonnie Dundee was not prepared to back off.

Despite being outnumbered two to one, the Highlanders launched a wild charge across the battlefield, an assault that swept away MacKay's men. The Battle of Killiecrankie was a significant victory for the Jacobites but Bonnie Dundee was killed in the exchanges and James had no-one to replace him. The legend of the terrifying Highlanders charge had been born, however, a legend that was to last until the final battle of the Jacobite era in 1746.

Defeat at the Battle of Dunkeld at the end of 1689, more of a street fight than a pitched contest on open ground, saw many of the clansmen give up and head home. An appeal for aid by Sir Ewan Cameron, who had taken command of the Jacobite army, brought no extra troops but James and Mary of Modena did send money, supplies and arms. It was too little, too late.

A night attack by government forces was launched on the remnants of Dundee's army at Cromdale on 30 April/1 May 1690. The result was complete victory for the Williamites with 400 Jacobites being put to the sword almost before they knew what was happening. It seemed as if the exile cause had foundered but, suddenly and unexpectedly, a remarkable Jacobite woman came to the fore. Her name was Grizzel Mhor Grant, the Lady Rothiemurchus.

* * *

Little is known about Grizzel Mhor Grant. Mhor was the name she was apparently given because of her great size. It is supposition but the deeds and appearance of Grizzel – a common enough name at the time – bears a striking resemblance to the later Welsh hero Jemima Nicholas, the town cobbler in Fishguard. The Welsh woman was known by the epithet Jemima Fawr and found fame a hundred years after Grizzel's activities in Scotland.

The word 'fawr' is Welsh for 'great' and is therefore not dis-similar to the descriptive term 'Mhor'. A French landing at Fishguard in 1797 during the French Revolutionary Wars saw Jemima take the lead in defence of the town. Single-handedly she captured a dozen French soldiers and was confirmed in Welsh legend as Jemima Fawr. The appellation Jemima Fawr was bestowed partly because of her great size and partly because of the enormity of her deed. The similarity to Grizzel Mhor is striking and leaves you to wonder if the people of Fishguard had heard of Grizzel's deeds and decided to create their own version.

What facts that are known about Grizzel Mhor are that she was born somewhere around 1620, the daughter of William Mackintosh of Kellachie and was married to James Grant of Rothiemurchus. She lived a long and, in the main, untroubled life. Prior to the Scottish risings of 1689, she was an active partner and wife of the local land owner, James Grant, well accepted and appreciated in the locality around Rothiemurchus. She and James had two sons, Patrick and William.

Grizzel remains one of those Jacobite women, like the nameless wives of crofters and farmers, who came to prominence for a moment or so during the various risings and then slipped back into oblivion. Even her name can be spelt in two different ways – two z's or one, take your choice.

Grizzel was no crofter's wife, however, and when in 1689 her husband, a confirmed Jacobite, set out to join the army of Bonnie Dundee she was left in charge of Loch-an-Eilean Castle. Like her husband Grizzel was a Jacobite through and through and while James Grant was serving with Dundee's army, her job was to keep the castle safe and out of Williamite hands.

The castle was set on the banks of the Loch. It was a beautiful and picturesque setting, more of a country house than a place or weapon of brutal war. But it was soon to face a challenge like it had never seen before.

Looking after the castle was a task that Grizzel performed well but the Jacobite cause in Scotland was doomed to failure. Bonnie Dundee's adventure was short-lived, hardly helped by his own death in battle, and never really gained the support it needed. And that, inevitably, spelt trouble for the remnants of the cause in the northern part of Scotland.

Following defeat at the Battle of Cromdale, a Williamite army arrived on the shore of Loch-an-Eilean and ordered the garrison in the castle to surrender. Grizzel replied the only way she knew. She slammed shut the castle gates – she would fight:

> The family of Rothiemurchus and some of their neighbours were obliged to take refuge in the castle, their own property. During their residence there they were attacked from the shore while a smart fire of musketry was kept up from the castle on the enemy which it required all of the men in the castle to carry on.[3]

Grizzel directed the defence of Loch-an-Eilean Castle but was not above lending her hand to the manual tasks such a defence required.

She apparently spent many hours casting lead musket balls to keep the defenders armed and ready.

In the end, the attacking Williamites decided that it would take too long and cost too much to continue the siege. They needed artillery to batter down the castle walls and siege guns were something they did not possess.

Losing faith in the enterprise, the Williamites simply abandoned their positions and headed off towards Inverness. Grizzel Mhor and her fellow defenders were able to relax again and the leader of the defence of Loch-an-Eilean Castle retired to obscurity.

One other story about Grizzel is worth telling, even though it has no Jacobite connections. However, it does reflect the character and fortitude of the woman who had successfully held out against government forces in 1690.

After the death of James Grant, things in the Rothiemurchus area began to change. The most significant development was that Patrick, the eldest son of James and Grizzel, took over the running of the family estates. He was young and enthusiastic but, like many land owners in post-Jacobite Scotland, he also had significant money worries.

As part of the arrangement giving him control of the Rothiemurchus estates, Patrick was ordered to compensate Grizzel with a sum of money as a pension each year, something that soon began to irk him and tug at his purse strings. To begin with, he consoled himself that Grizzel would not be around forever but, unfortunately for him, his mother lived to an advanced old age and Patrick began to wonder if she would ever die. Perhaps God had forgotten her, he thought.

And so, he decided to act. It may have been unkind, brutal even, but Grizzel Mhor would probably have approved, as long as it wasn't being done to her!

Patrick duly had the aged Grizzel carried to the top of a nearby hill, placing her, as he declared, nearer to Heaven than she had ever been before. Grizzel Mhor was not ready to die, however, and survived the outing, seemingly none the worse for her exposure to the elements. After a few hours in the wind and rain, they had to carry Grizzel back down. She continued to live for several more years, happily draining Patrick's pockets to the end.[4]

* * *

Defeat at Dundalk and Cromdale in 1689 and 1690 had effectively ended the Jacobite rebellion in Scotland, at least for the time being. James, safely back in France, slipped slowly but inevitably into a senile old age, haunted by what he had lost and seemed never likely to regain. The Jacobite cause was not dead, however. What it needed was a martyr – or, better still, several of them. And the infamous Massacre of Glencoe gave the Jacobites exactly that.

The massacre has long been assumed to be part of the MacDonald-Campbell feud that had been going on for years. In fact, clan warfare in the Highlands had already misted into past history. What was left consisted of banditry on a local level and some elements of petty lawbreaking. Annoying to the authorities it may have been but it hardly warranted such a dramatic response as the Massacre of Glencoe.[5]

The massacre was actually a carefully planned event, directed by the English Government with Sir John Dalrymple, Secretary of State for Scotland, as the main player. A die-hard Protestant who hated the Catholic clans and saw the MacDonalds as a particular threat to peace in Scotland, Dalrymple was undoubtedly the 'evil genius' behind the killings.

The trigger for the massacre was a pardon issued to the Jacobites by King William, provided they took an oath of allegiance to him by 1 January 1692. It was a generous offer, one that even the exiled James II agreed should be accepted. Chief MacLain of the MacDonalds received the news late in December and set off for Fort William to take the oath on behalf of his clan.

With Christmas and Hogmanay still being celebrated, MacLain was shunted from pillar to post, trying to find officials to take his oath and it was not until 2 January that he was able to stand in front of the Sheriff of Argyll to pledge allegiance to King William. Technically he was beyond the official closing date which had been set for the oath-taking and it remains hard not to believe that he had been deliberately kept waiting.

Deliberate delay or not, Sir John Dalrymple now ordered 120 soldiers, all Campbells from the Argyll Regiment of Foot, to the pass of Glencoe. The valley and surrounding area was traditional MacDonald territory and the arrival of redcoats did not sit easily with the locals. Even so, there was an uneasy but increasingly acceptable period of calm. Put simply and despite all fears, the soldiers and the members of the MacDonald clan seemed to get on reasonably well.

For two weeks the soldiers waited, billeted with the families of the MacDonalds, sharing their food and their leisure activities. Legend declares that many of them even occupied the beds, not instead of but along with, female members of the rival clan.

Finally, Robert Campbell, officer in charge of the soldiers, received a message from London. It was signed by the King but was undoubtedly the work of John Dalrymple:

> You are hereby ordered to fall upon the rebels, the MacDonalds of Glencoe and put to the sword all under seventy. You are to take special care that the old fox and his sons do upon no account escape your hands.[6]

The order, accompanied by threats about what would happen to Campbell if the instructions were not explicitly followed, was duly executed early in the morning of 13 February 1692. Soldiers burst through the doors of houses where they had been made to feel so welcome over the past few weeks and dragged women and children outside into the snow. Men were callously killed where they stood, Chief MacLaine being despatched while rising from his bed, shot in the back.

In all, thirty-eight of the MacDonalds were killed outright, many more, mostly women and children, dying from exposure in the pass of Glencoe. The exact total of deaths has never been properly recorded. Numbers were irrelevant; it was the event that was important as far as Dalrymple and others were concerned.

Several instances of mercy were shown by some of the Campbell soldiers, helping women and children to escape, firing into the air above the heads of running men and so on, but such stories were deliberately kept hidden. That was not what Dalrymple and his minions wanted from the massacre.

News of the killings spread quickly, giving new fire and depth to the Jacobite movement. The Campbells were seen as the villains, at least by the Scots, and vilified by the majority of the Highland clans. Even Sir John Dalrymple did not escape censure.

An inquiry was held in 1696, the conclusion being that the massacre was an act of wilful murder. Dalrymple was forced to resign – although he soon reappeared in a more senior position – and the affair passed into Scottish history and legend.

The massacre gave the Jacobite cause exactly the boost it needed at a moment when support for the exiled James seemed to be waning or dying away. It had been an opportune disaster, something that the Jacobites seized eagerly.

Bonnie Dundee's rising in 1690 had not been anywhere as popular as he had wished, fewer than 2000 men joining his army. In 1715, admittedly some years after Glencoe, the rising led by the Earl of Mar saw the Jacobites raise a force of over 10,000. That leaves the rhetorical question – would such support have been quite so forthcoming for Mar's rebellion if the Massacre of Glencoe had not taken place?

After the Glencoe Massacre the Jacobite cause and, by default, the Catholic religion to which many of the Highlanders subscribed, were more popular than ever. Dundee's rising had clearly been too early, another 'what if' in the chapter of Scottish and Jacobite history.

* * *

Apart from Mary of Modena and Grizzel Mhor Grant little is known about the women of the early Jacobite risings. The all-encompassing veil of anonymity that affects so many minor characters in history has cloaked them and kept most of them hidden from public view. Even now, several hundred years after the last Jacobite rising, it remains an infuriating fault of history. And yet it was not something that happened merely by chance. The anonymity was aided and abetted by society's attitude to women in the seventeenth and eighteenth centuries, protective and dismissive at the same time.

Throughout what has been called the 'early modern period' there was a distinct impression that men and women were viewed on an equal footing when it came to participation in riot or affray. As magistrates and protectors of the law knew only too well, both sexes were more than capable of taking matters into their own hands when they felt the occasion demanded it.

The writer Robert Southey took a more distinct and dramatic view, straying perhaps into the land of cliché, a realm where 'the female of the species is always more deadly than the male':

> Southey held it a commonplace that women are far more likely to be mutinous; "they stand in less fear of the law, partly from ignorance, partly because they presume upon

the privilege of their sex, and therefore in all public tumults they are foremost in violence and ferocity."[7]

Like all good cliches, there is an element of truth about Southey's words. As an example, several disturbances in the reign of Henry VIII had been led solely by women and even the anti-Anne Boleyn faction of the 1530s created an anger that was initiated and conducted mainly by jealous members of the female sex. And so it continued, long after Henry VIII was dead, women being powerful elements in many of the anti-social activities of the sixteenth and seventeenth centuries.

However, when riots and disturbances were put down and 'justice' was meted out, women were almost always absent from any subsequent legal involvement. The regularity of women's involvement in disturbances in big cities, in villages and in the countryside excludes the possibility of such happenstance, such exclusions being purely by chance.

It has never been made totally clear why these exclusions should be the case. It is possible that women were protected by their men folk, anxious not to lose economically valuable partners and the mothers of their children. Love, rarely spoken about in working class environments during this time, may also have played a significant part.

At times of riot and outright physical protest, unlike their male counterparts, women may also have had the good sense to slip away from the crowd once the initial outburst was over and things began to go wrong. Self-control, however, was never at the forefront of anyone's mind, male or female, when the Riot Act was read and blood was up.

It is far more likely that women were, in a strange and somewhat ill-defined manner, protected by the legal systems of the time. It is, in part, supposition or guess work but an ill-formed attitude of society in general probably had much to do with what was really a shielding process and a distinct bending of the rules:

> There does seem to have been a widespread conviction – there was certainly no explicit corpus of law to confirm it – that a woman could participate in riot without being legally pursued at law.[8]

In the early eighteenth century, that approach or belief was an interpretation of prevailing justice which was openly and freely accepted in Britain and in countries like France and Holland. Only in matters like witchcraft was there an automatic decision to prosecute women who came before the Bench. That was a decision that cost the lives of somewhere in the region of 20,000 to 30,000 women across Europe in a period of 200 years.

For 'ordinary' riot and civil disturbance, the more protective approach was invariably taken. With the difference between riot and rebellion somewhat blurred, there appears to have been an accepted fact that while women were certainly capable of anti-social acts, they needed to be shielded from the worst effects of their personalities and intentions. They were commonly regarded and often spoken about as 'the weaker sex'; defence of their actions, often unbridled and uncontrolled, was therefore natural and expected.

Magistrates would very often 'weed out' female offenders, usually before trials or legal hearings even began. The rationale behind such positive discrimination remains unclear although it was possibly as simple as a means to reduce the number of dependent children that the town or county would have to care for if their mothers were suddenly taken away.

Whatever the rationale, as far as the Jacobite rebellions and uprisings were concerned, the absence of legal proceedings against women, particularly women of the lower or working classes, helped to keep them hidden from public view. That undoubtedly protected them at the time but it has also continued to weave the blanket of obscurity where Jacobite women are concerned.

One more factor to be considered when looking at the roles of women during the various risings is the paternalistic attitude of men, particularly men of the economically secure mid-range variety, men of standing and position in society.

These men were invariably anti-Jacobite in their political stance. Writers like Henry Fielding and Samuel Johnson, Whigs to the bone, perfectly caught the image of the hard-drinking, corpulent Tory or Jacobite gentleman, pipe in hand, spewing out bonhomie and good fellowship – but only for men. The pictures they created were satirical but always tinged with a degree of reality.

Fielding's Squire Weston in *Tom Jones* is clear about the situation when he declares to his sister that politics belong to men, noting that 'petticoats should not meddle'. Comedic now, hard-edged reality back then. Johnson was always more direct:

"A man is in general better pleased when he has a good dinner upon his table than when his wife talks Greek," is a well-known Johnson aphorism.[9]

Sexist, patronising, the attitudes of both Whigs and Tories came down to the belief that a woman's place was clearly in the home. It was an attitude that was mirrored in the Scottish clan system and was another reason for the seeming absence of Jacobite women in the early risings.

With a population of around 600,000, in the late seventeenth century the Highlands of Scotland were dominated by the clan system. If the clansmen were not all related to each other they certainly believed they were but that did not stop them raiding and rustling the cattle of their near-neighbours, something which at times seemed to be their chief occupation. Antipathy between the clans, particularly the Campbells who seemed to be universally hated, was generally quite common and did sometimes flare up in violence.

The clan chief, the most important figure in each of the clan villages, was not the rustic, brutal and barbaric figure of legend. In fact, most chiefs were well-educated, able to speak Gaelic, English, even French and Latin. His wife was treated like a lady and, with her husband often away on raiding parties or herding and selling cattle, she had almost as much authority as her husband – an important factor in the forthcoming events of the Jacobite era.[10]

Most women from the clans, however, occupied a much lower position in the hierarchy and the pecking order. In what was really a militaristic society, their place, just as Fielding and Johnson had decreed for English women, lay in the home. That was where they belonged and that was where they must stay.

It took a very enlightened man indeed to view women and their place in the world differently, just as it took a particularly dynamic and determined woman to break the shackles of what was, in effect, the last remnants of serfdom. Men went off to war, women remained behind to tend cattle and prepare to dress the wounds of their menfolk when they returned.

Of course, there were exceptions and things were beginning to change, all over the British Isles. The image of women stealing onto the battlefield to nurse and tend to wounded Highlanders is not far removed from the truth. The annoying factor is that so many of them have remained anonymous.

Chapter Four

Yet More Chances

Along with the military disasters in Scotland, defeat for the Jacobites at the Battle of the Boyne had made the new English monarchs, William III and Mary II, more than a little content and secure on their thrones. Immediate threats were gone and what remained, for the whole of the British Isles, was a unique situation.

The Protestant succession seemed secure and for the first time, there were joint sovereigns on the English throne. More significantly, however, the 1701 Act of Settlement ensured that every monarch who came after them – Queen Anne and all of the Hanoverian Georges – reigned, not by sovereign right but by invitation from Parliament.

Erosion of royal power was inevitably accompanied by an increase in Parliamentary control but that did not happen overnight. It took time for the new system to become bedded in and inevitably there were mistakes and teething troubles. The military challenge of Jacobitism might, for the moment, be marginalised but unrest and discontent still seethed in the country.

That was particularly apparent in the field of religion and in Scotland it was more noticeable than in most other parts of the country. While some of the Highland clans were intent on remaining with the Catholicism of their past, most other Scots were staunch believers and followers of the Presbyterian religion that had been in place since the Reformation of Henry VIII.

There were pockets of practicing Episcopalians and in many respects, the Scottish Episcopalian Church, small as it might be, was not dissimilar from the larger Anglican religion of England. The Episcopalian congregations rejected the authority of the Pope but imbued their Bishops with much of the power previously held by Rome. Like Anglicanism, it rejected many of the Catholic rituals, particularly the communion which the Episcopalians regarded as a symbolic process rather than an actual changing of bread and wine into the body and blood of Christ.

An English Parliamentary decision dating to 1690 provided an attempt to enforce an Episcopalian settlement on the Scottish people and on their church. In line with the Anglican religion of England, it promised uniformity of faith and a move even further away from the dreaded Catholicism so beloved by James. It was, however, both ill-judged and ill-timed and, given the political mood of the country, was an unnecessary affliction for the Scottish people.

The Presbyterian Church was looked on fondly by Scots from the Lowlands and also from several parts of the Highlands which meant that the new settlement was daunting for those who had to implement the Episcopalian system but nothing short of horrifying for those who were subjected to it. The Episcopalians and Presbyterians in Scotland had merged or at least managed to live side by side since the time of the Restoration in 1660. If nothing else, this new direction was bound to break them apart once more.

The ghost of John Knox and his strict Presbyterian values still hovered in the background and there was no way the Scots were going to easily accept what was really an alien intrusion into their beliefs. The short-sighted piece of legislation was bound to create tensions.

King William was aware of the dangers but he was pressurised by Parliament and by his government to impose the settlement. As William feared, in consequence, many of the established clergy in Scotland refused to accept the change, viewing the imposition of a 'foreign' religion and the abolition of Bishops that accompanied it as a tyrannical act on behalf of the English state.

Over half of the Scottish clergy promptly declined to take the Oath of Allegiance to William and Mary. These refusers became known as Nonjurors.

For Nonjurors and for most Episcopalians the hereditary principle of the monarchy was crucial and by swearing the Oath of Allegiance to William and Mary they believed that they would be going against all their beliefs and values. Those beliefs centred on total submission to the authority of the monarch and they had already sworn an oath to King James. Doing the same to William and Mary, imposed on them while James was still alive, would be nothing short of sacrilege.

Nevertheless, the English government insisted on the Oath being taken by the ministers and all church members. In its own way, that decision was as reckless as King James' 1687 Declaration of Indulgence which had suspended all laws against Catholics – morally correct, politically self-destructive. It would inevitably lead to problems in the realm.

By imposing the Presbyterian settlement on the Scottish people, the English government had done little more than push their clergy into the arms of the Jacobites. And there they became hugely significant.

In order for any movement, political or spiritual, to survive and flourish there needed, then and now, to be an ideology beneath the surface impression and public face of any public body or belief. The Nonjurors quickly became the men who gave that ideological basis to the Jacobite cause, probably even more so than the Catholics who have always been seen as sitting at the root of Jacobitism, both in belief and cause.

It is estimated that 15 of the 26 Highland clans which gathered to fight or support the Jacobite cause during the rising of '15 were Episcopalian, five were of mixed denomination and only six were loyal to the Catholic faith.[1] The traditional view of the Jacobite revolts where the conflicts consisted mainly of struggles and combats between Lowlanders and Highlanders, Catholics and Protestants, the Campbells against everyone else, simply does not hold water. The makeup of the clan army gives a somewhat different slant on motivation to the Jacobite struggles.

Despite the significant number of Presbyterians and Episcopalians in Scotland the influence of the Catholic faith remained strong, as Walter Scott noted in *Rob Roy*, one of his early historical novels based around the time of the 1715 Jacobite rising:

> "He is what we call a very clever man in this country, where clever men are scarce. Bred to the church, but in no hurry to take orders."
> "To the Catholic Church?"
> "The Catholic Church! What church else?"[2]

Penal laws had been re-introduced in 1689, during the first year of William and Mary's reign. It left the Catholics in Britain with little recourse but to look to the exiled Stuarts for help and religious toleration. And with the implementation of the Presbyterian settlement that meant, in Scotland, Ireland and in some parts of Wales, the Jacobite movement, although temporarily on the back foot, could only gain in strength and value.

* * *

The final years of the seventeenth and the early part of the eighteenth centuries saw a slow but steady growth in support for the Jacobites. It was not a mass rising or invasion but, rather, feelings and emotions that manifested themselves in little things like men and women meeting in secret and toasting *The King Over the Water.* The toast was made over a bowl of water or, occasionally, a finger bowl in the centre of the table. After the death of William III, another salutation became popular in Jacobite circles – *To The Little Gentleman in Black.*

This latter toast owed its origin to an accident that befell King William and led to his death in 1702. Out riding, William's horse Sorrel stumbled on a mole hill. William was thrown from his saddle and broke his collar bone. The fall from his horse did not kill him but pneumonia set in and, within a few short weeks, the King died, hence the Jacobite praise for *the Little Gentleman in Black.*

Various alternative versions of the toast were in common usage, *The Little Gentleman in the Black Velvet Waistcoat* and so on. It was hardly rebellious stuff, even though such toasts were officially treasonable comments. Turning a blind eye was the standard government response.

A number of Jacobite societies sprang up across Britain during this time. Groups such as *The Circle of Gentlemen, The Independent Gentlemen of Westminster* and *The '15* met on a regular basis to 'talk treason' and enjoy a good night out with plenty of food and wine. Indeed, the hearty 'Hail fellow, well met' attitude of the Jacobite societies seems now to have been the driving force behind their creation. Most, if not all, of the Jacobite societies were male-dominated, those organisations that did admit women consigning them to things like preparing food for the male members to enjoy.[3]

The Whig government kept a close watch on the societies but did not, in general, pursue or disperse them. It was far easier to have all the Jacobite supporters, most of them corpulent country gentlemen who would have been hardly able to mount a horse, let alone fight, in one place. Apart from anything else they were thought to be harmless, an impression proven by the fact that groups like *The Cycle of the White Rose* even kept minutes of their meetings – hardly the most sinister of anti-government secret societies.

Queen Mary had died in 1694, leaving William alone and heartbroken. Her death, as the only one of the two monarchs who had direct and sovereign right to the throne, did not cause the problems it might have done. The idea of an invited monarch had already become more significant than any birth right.

William struggled on until his riding accident in 1702 and was succeeded, as the 1701 Act of Settlement had declared, by his sister-in-law Anne. She was the daughter of James II and sister to Queen Mary, the last of the Stuart monarchs, but her accession had been approved by Parliament.

Relations between the legislative bodies of England and Scotland were notoriously bad and with the coming of Queen Anne, there was growing support on both sides of the border for a more clearly defined unity between the two countries. Anne duly appointed commissioners to examine the problem and come up with a solution. It took just three months and the Act of Union, incorporating England and Scotland under the name Great Britain, came into effect on 1 May 1707.

There were benefits and drawbacks to the hastily contrived solution to the problem. On the plus side, the Act secured the Protestant succession in both countries and trade between them was made free and equal without undue taxation and custom duties. As Scotland was in desperate need of economic security and material help, the fact that a large portion of England's National Debt was passed on to the nation north of the border failed to make much of an impact.

The poor nature of Scotland's economy was given as one reason for limiting the number of Scottish members in the House of Commons to just 45, sixteen in the House of Lords. In hindsight, it seems a strange ruling and the Scots did not accept it easily.

Perhaps the most significant clause in the Act of Union concerned religion. The Scottish Presbyterian and the English Episcopalian Churches were secured against change, a decision that pleased many but left the hard-liners adrift and wondering.

* * *

The Act of Settlement had been passed in June 1701 while William was still alive. By the terms of this piece of legislation, if either William or his planned successor Anne died without heirs, the throne would pass to Sophia of Hanover, the granddaughter of the original Stuart monarch, James I. If Sophia was dead it would go to her heirs, on the proviso that they were Protestants. It was a logical move for the Protestant English administrators but, strangely, it was also a ruling that gave a much-needed boost to Catholic Jacobite supporters.

Catholics had hoped that, on the death of Anne, the crown would be returned to the deposed Catholic monarch James II or his descendants. Clearly, now, that was not going to happen. There was only one way to return Britain to the arms of Catholicism – by replacing the existing system of sovereigns with the exiled Stuart family. James II might be dead but his son, the would-be James III, the Old Pretender, was alive and kicking. Jacobite support went up by at least a good notch or two.

There had been several plots to kill or assassinate William, notably the Aylesbury Plot of 1691 and the Fenwick Plot of 1695. The latter plot had been accompanied by serious Jacobite rioting in London and for a while the country was plagued by an invasion scare. Habeas corpus was even suspended for some time. Nothing came of the scare and it was March 1708 that the next significant threat to the English crown took place.

The invasion plan of 1708 was a French idea, known as the Enterprise d'Ecosse. But right from the beginning it was clear that although it might be a combined operation, the French and the Jacobites had vastly different aims.

The Jacobites were intent on one thing – returning the crown of England to the Old Pretender and his family. And the French? For them it was simply a way of diverting English attention away from the War of the Spanish Succession which was then raging in Europe. The Duke of Marlborough's victories in Flanders and the Low Countries had put the French on the back foot and they needed to regain their position of strength. If an invasion threat could force the British government to pull Marlborough and his troops, some of them at least, back from the Continent it would be well worth the gamble.

From the beginning of the operation, however, things went wrong and as the plan began to unravel nobody seemed to have the sense or the ability to change direction or call it a day. When the decision was finally made to abandon the enterprise, it was far too late to escape with any remaining vestiges of pride and dignity.

James, the Pretender, was to be there but for the voyage across the Channel and North Sea, he was to be just a passenger. The expedition was led by Count Claude de Forbin and by his second-in-command, the operation's military leader, Comte de Gace. Neither of them had much faith in the project, so much so that they seized every opportunity to prevaricate and delay. Eventually, they had to be forced to sail after a threatening letter from King Louis.

It was, in many respects, a rather flippant plan. A fleet of 30 fast privateers had been converted into transports by removing their guns and cutting down crews to the bare minimum. Speed was essential to the success of the plan but, once the conversions were complete, it was obvious that if fate should happen to throw the invading force into the path of the enemy, the French fleet would be no match for the British Navy.

James III, the nineteen-year-old son of the recently dead James II, joined the expedition at Dunkirk on 9 March 1708. He was excited at the prospect of reclaiming his dead father's throne but, from the beginning of the enterprise, he was faced with a series of problems.

By now 5000 French soldiers were on board the ships, all eager and waiting to get started. However, the off-shore presence of the British Admiral George Byng, patrolling the waters around Gravelines, prevented the French from sailing for two weeks. With their under-manned and lightly armoured privateers, Forbin and Gace did not dare to face the British squadron. The men of the expeditionary force waited and fumed.

Then James caught measles and Forbin decided that everything must be further delayed. Spitting and cursing, the soldiers disembarked and headed for the nearest taverns. James lay on his sick bed, equally as frustrated. The only ones happy and content with the situation were Forbin and Gace.

And then fate seemingly played into the French and Jacobite hands. By sheer good fortune for the French, Admiral Byng out in the waters off Dunkirk was, first, blown westwards by contrary winds and then forced to return to England to take on fresh supplies for his Royal Navy squadron. It was a window of opportunity.

James recovered from his measles within a few short weeks, the French soldiers re-embarked and, now untroubled by the enemy, the invasion fleet sailed. King Louis XIV of France was there to see them go. Apparently, his last words to the Old Pretender were simple and straight to the point: 'The best wish I can make you is that I never see your face again.'[4]

Once they had been put ashore, James and his troops were supposed to meet up with a Jacobite army raised by Sir Patrick Maule, the Earl of Panmure. He had promised a rising of 25,000 Highlanders to fight alongside the French, always a highly optimistic, not to say deceitful, estimate.

In the end, a much smaller Scottish force gathered on the coast and waited. As it turned out the Scots were not called on to fight. There was no link-up with James and the longer the Scottish army kicked their heels the likelihood of discovery and disaster grew. Finally, with defeat staring them in the face, the members of the Scottish Jacobite army had the good sense to slip away, back to their homes.

The Earl of Panmure, who was later to lose his title after his involvement in the '15 Rising, could do nothing to stop them. The clansmen had already spent long enough kicking their heels and, for the moment at least, Panmure seemed to have got away with treason.

Almost as soon as the invasion fleet sailed, severe storms blew in – not the first time Britain had been saved by inclement weather. The converted privateers were built for speed, not stability, and James, along with most of the soldiers, suffered badly from sea-sickness.

Battling all the way against the gales, the invasion fleet eventually made landfall far to the north of their proposed landing site in the Firth of Forth. Forbin eventually managed to anchor off Fife Ness and despite there being no sight of the promised Highland battalions, James prepared to disembark.

Before the Old Pretender and his French army could step onto Scottish soil, however, Admiral Byng appeared over the horizon with his squadron. James pleaded to be put ashore, knowing that he had more chance of success on dry land than he ever did at sea.

Forbin refused – there was not enough time, he declared. Byng's powerful warships would be on them before the job was half completed. And so, the French hauled in their anchors and fled north, the only direction that was left to them. They tried to get into the Moray Firth but wind and tides were against them.

Claude de Forbin knew when he was beaten. Choosing his moment, he slipped past Byng and headed back to France, pursued all the way by Byng's better-armed and vastly superior ships of war. There were a number of short engagements between the two fleets and the French vessels suffered considerable damage. Many of the soldiers were killed but the remnants of the invading force eventually made it back to Dunkirk.

Queen Anne breathed a sigh of relief and, despite not being renowned for her wit or quick tongue, derisively bestowed on James the title of 'Old Mr Misfortunate' The appellation hit the mark with supporters from both sides and the nickname stuck!

Once the dust had settled on the affair, it was obvious that James, the Pretender, was back in France where his dreams, his plans and his adventure, where everything had begun. It might not have been what he wanted but the country was, at least, hospitable. And maybe his stay would be for something of an extended period.

King Louis' wish had not come true and he would have to entertain James and his Jacobite entourage for a little while longer.

In fact, it would be seven long years before James III would finally manage to get ashore in Britain. Even to an out-and-out detester of England and all she stood for, it was becoming clear to Louis XIV that he was harbouring something of a poisoned chalice!

Chapter Five

The '15 Rising: Jacobite Women Flex Their Muscles

By the time of the 1715 rising the Jacobite cause had been strengthened by a large outpouring of anti-Union emotion amongst the Scottish people. The 1707 Act of Union with England had lost whatever popularity it may once have held. And that was small enough, however you looked at it. Now, the inequalities which soon became glaringly obvious finally prompted strong Nationalist feelings from the Scots.

In 1710, with feelings already running high, there had been an unexpected change in the English government. The Tories, who were felt by many to be secret plotters or schemers – possibly even direct and open supporters – for the return of the original Stuart dynasty replaced the Whigs as the governing party at Westminster.

It was a revolutionary change in direction for British Parliamentary politics which for some time had been the preserve of the progressive Whig majority. Whigs and Hanoverians, the two had always seemed to go together but now, once more, a return to the days of pre-Glorious Revolution seemed to be on the cards. What price a reinstatement of the exiled Stuart monarchy, people began to ask?

The Tories might not have come out directly asking for a return to the days of James II but the idea was still there, spoken about in hushed whispers in the coffee houses and at Jacobite meetings, underlying much of the country's policy and debate. The idea was treasonable and therefore simply added to the confusion of Jacobite-era politics.

When this hotch-potch of unhappiness was mixed with or joined by strong Jacobite support in the North-East of England it appeared to many thinking people that James, the Pretender, was finally about to come into his own. Did he have the desire, people asked, to make a positive move? Did he have the nerve to front up a challenge to the aging Queen Anne?

It was, indeed, a dilemma for James. The north country support was based on Episcopalianism and, therefore, on a firm belief in the return of the hereditary nature of the monarchy. That suited James but it was offset by the still relatively new powers that had been given to Parliament during the reign of William and Mary.

The bottom line was really very simple – was there a logical desire to replace the existing Stuart monarchs with the original Stuarts, the rightful dynasty? Putting the son of the exiled King James on the throne of England was suddenly a distinct possibility. Or was it?

There was no system, no way of achieving such a result other than by open rebellion and by victory on the battlefield. And, for the moment at least, the higher echelons of the Jacobite/Tory grouping showed no inclination to fight another costly invasion campaign. As the months ran by the situation only seemed more and more confusing, even dangerous for Queen Anne and the ruling dynasty.

Queen Anne died in 1714 and before anyone could do or say anything different, George I, Elector of Hanover, duly succeeded to the English throne. He was actually 52nd in line but as the 51 individuals above him were all Catholics they were automatically disbarred from taking the crown.

George was still in Hanover when he heard about the death of Anne and emissaries had to be sent to swiftly bring the new King back to his new domain. According to legend and folklore, he was digging vegetables in his garden when the news was relayed to him. Happy to take the crown, he was not so content with actually taking up residence in the British Isles.

George spoke no English, had no affinity with any of the Home Nations and from the start was decidedly unpopular. If ever there was an appropriate moment for James III to appear and claim the throne this was it. But he did nothing. It was another missed opportunity for the Jacobites and instead of appearing in London or any of the other centres of population, in June 1714 the new Hanoverian regime put a price of £5000 – soon raised to £10,000 – on his head.[1]

The new King had come to England, people said, for the money and for the glory of kingship. He had come for the security provided by the English throne. He had come for – what had he come for? Many people did not have the slightest idea why George had come and the rumble of discontent could be heard all over Europe. It was a second opportunity within a few months for the Jacobites and, if they could gear themselves into action this was the time to strike.

The '15 Rising: Jacobite Women Flex Their Muscles

Everything seemed to be falling into place. The French duly offered assistance, presenting the Jacobites with money and supplies, and even allowed James brief access to French soil. They detailed a few regiments of soldiers to join the expedition but their help stopped there, innate French caution obliging them to stop, think and leave the actual fighting to the Jacobites.

The original plan was for a three-pronged attack on Britain, the main assault coming in the West Country. Two other incursions would take place in the North of England and in Scotland. These were to be little more than diversionary attacks, designed to pull defensive forces away from Cornwall and Devon. What happened, however, was a perfect example of the poor communication that be-devilled the relationships between the Jacobites in Britain and those exiled on the Continent.

The rebellion in the South-West was crushed before it even began. Spies within the Jacobite movement gave the authorities the names of the main movers and their intentions. The Hanoverian government swooped and, with their leaders kicking their heels in prison, the threat from the West Country Jacobites simply faded away.

James and his Continental allies were not informed, however. The Old Pretender, then living in Loraine, got as far as St Malo where he waited for several weeks with his small contingent of French soldiers while yet more bad weather battered the Channel ports. He was still not told of the disaster in England.

When James did finally get the news, he disguised himself as a sailor – the terms of the Treaty of Utrecht had forbidden him to set foot in France – and headed for Dunkirk. His intention, now, was to turn the secondary risings in Scotland and the North into the main assaults.

John Erskine, the Earl of Mar, was the acknowledged leader of the Scottish rising. He had already declared for James, raising the Jacobite standard at Braemar on 27 August but, unfortunately for the Jacobites, that was about all he did manage to do.

Over the next few weeks, Mar waited. He kicked his heels, prevaricated and failed to take advantage of a 5 to 1 numerical superiority over the Whig general, John Campbell, the Duke of Argyll. He did manage to capture the town of Perth and one or two other Scottish cities but failed to take Edinburgh and his issuing of a proclamation ordering the landlords in his army to pay a large levy towards Jacobite funds did not go down well.

When the two armies did finally come face to face at Sheriffmuir, Mar had command of nearly five thousand men; Argyll, by contrast had barely 3000. The battle was a badly conducted affair with both sides unwilling to press home their advantage or to risk failure. The one notable event during Sheriffmuir was Argyll's counter attack in the early stages of the battle, an action that stopped in its tracks the famed charge of the Highlanders.

With darkness both forces withdrew, each of them claiming to be the winners. In fact, despite losing more men than the Jacobites, it was a government victory, Argyll having prevented Mar from heading further south and investing Edinburgh:

> The famous Rob Roy watched the battle with his MacGregors from a vantage point a mile away, waiting to see which side would be victorious. Of Mar he is reported to have said: "If he cannot win without me, then he will not win with me."[2]

Further disasters for the Jacobites occurred on the same day as the Battle of Sheriffmuir, 13 November 1715. The town of Inverness and other recently acquired Scottish territories were lost and the clansmen in the Earl of Mar's army began to drift away.

The Earl of Derwentwater, commander of the Jacobites in northern England, had decided to head south, leaving Mar to his own devices. It was a mistake that left both English and Scottish Jacobite forces adrift rather than uniting in one army to confront the Hanoverians. That winter Derwentwater and his forces settled and created a defensive position in the town of Preston.

The Battle of Preston where Northern Jacobites ventured onto the field of combat for the first time was a hard-fought contest with heavy casualties on both sides. It was a battle that was eventually won by government forces.

In fact, Preston was more of a street fight than a formal battle, snipers and arson being two of the main weapons used by both sides. It has since laid claim, which many argue is a dubious contention, to be the last battle fought on English soil. To the Jacobites that was irrelevant, they had lost the advantage that had clearly been theirs.

By the time James landed at Peterhead in December, it was almost all over. A potentially powerful opportunity had been wasted by indecision and by the woeful lack of clear command. James was on British soil, however, and that in itself was something of a triumph for him.

Unlike his father and, in due course, his son Charles, James was no general and certainly no great leader. Personal charm apart, he came with no real idea of what to do, how to rectify a doomed situation. Almost immediately after landing at Peterhead, his health broke down and when, at the beginning of 1716, news that the Spanish treasure ship which was bringing him much-needed gold and silver had run ashore off Dundee, he was mortified.

Over the next few months, there was considerable manoeuvring and marching by the troops of both sides but James did not see it. On 4 February he and the Earl of Mar had embarked on a ship and sailed back to France. The 1715 Rising, the only Jacobite incursion to operate without foreign planning or involvement, was effectively over.

* * *

So, what about the Jacobite women during the '15 rising? They were certainly active during the campaign and they, at least, emerged with some credit from a disastrous attempt to place James III on the throne. There were many camp followers, tagging onto the Earl of Mar's army, ordinary women from the crofts and farmhouses who performed the duties of caring for the sick and wounded. But there were also several women of real consequence and social standing. They were named in the press and in history, both at the time and in the future.

One of the most famous was the Countess of Nithsdale, Lady Nithsdale as she was known. Born Winifred Maxwell, daughter of the Catholic nobleman Lord Powis, she met her future husband at the French court when her father, a prominent Jacobite, was in exile. William Maxwell, the 5th Earl of Nithsdale, was visiting to pay his respects to the deposed King. The relationship between him and Winifred grew and, a few years later in 1699, they were married.

Nithsdale was one of a number of Scottish noblemen arrested after the Jacobite defeat at Preston and jailed for his part in the '15 Rising. Found guilty of treason, he was sentenced to death and placed in the Tower of London to await his fate. Lady Nithsdale heard about the sentence in December 1715 and, despite her supposed 'delicate' constitution, she became determined and furious in her desire to set him free. She saddled her horse and along with Cecilia Evans, her maid, braved the bitterly cold winter weather to ride south to Newcastle.

From Newcastle, Winifred and Cecilia took a coach across country to York, the hub of all transport south. By now it was snowing heavily and the London coach was delayed. Undaunted and knowing that time was of the essence, Lady Nithsdale hired a string of horses and the two women set off, without help or escort, for Westminster.

The journey was long and arduous, Winifred and her maid having to halt for a while at Stamford because their horses were nearly buried in snow. They arrived at their destination in January 1716. Once in London and safely lodged with the supportive Mrs Mills of Drury Lane, Henrietta collapsed; it took several days to get her fit and well again.

As soon as she was able, however, it was time to make the first overtures for the release of her husband and a grimly determined Lady Nithsdale headed for the palace at Westminster. Once she arrived at the palace, Winifred pushed aside the flunkeys and court officials, demanding to see the King. Unable to stop her, the officials were pushed aside and had no option but to admit her into George's presence.

In a letter written to her sister a few years later, Lady Nithsdale described what happened when she came into the King's presence. If her description is accurate, it gives a good impression of Winifred's character and her determination to set her husband free. She was certainly undaunted by the presence of King George:

> I threw myself at his feet and told him in French that I was the unfortunate Countess of Nithsdale.[3]

She spoke better French than George, whose only real language was German, and that may have influenced his response to Winifred's pleas. He immediately made to leave the room and her presence:

> I caught hold of the skirt of his coat and he dragged me on my knees from the middle of the room to the very door of the drawing room ... I almost fainted away from grief and disappointment.[4]

Lady Nithsdale was pulled away from the King by his attendants, the petition she had been intending to present to George dropping to the

The '15 Rising: Jacobite Women Flex Their Muscles

floor. Realising that there was no chance of a pardon for her husband, she left the palace and began to put the final stages of an alternative escape plan into operation.

Along with Winifred's maid, another two Jacobite women were now drawn into the plot. These were Mrs Mills, the landlady of the house where the Countess was lodging, and a friend who is sometimes referred to as Mrs Morgan, sometimes as Miss Hilton.

Over a period of the next few weeks, Winifred visited her husband in the Tower on several occasions. The guards quickly came to like and admire her, gratefully accepting the money she gave them to 'drink the King's health' Then, on 23 February 1716, the eve of Earl Nithsdale's planned execution, Winfred, Mrs Mills and Mrs Morgan visited him for what was supposedly the last time.

Knowing that only two visitors at a time were allowed in to see the Earl, Winifred introduced and took in the slim Mrs Morgan. Today, however, Mrs Morgan looked rather fat. The guards noted the fact but did not challenge the pair.

Once in the cell, Mrs Morgan took off her outer garments to disclose a second set of clothes, all intended for Mrs Mills hidden beneath them. There were also several other garments that would be needed. Items of her own garments were passed over and left behind for the Earl. When a seemingly distraught Mrs Morgan left the Tower, it was the turn of Mrs Mills to play her part in the escape. Lady Nithsdale had everything planned and knew exactly what to do next:

> I went partly down stairs to meet Mrs Mills who had taken the precaution to hold her handkerchief to her face, as was very natural for a woman to do when she was going to bid her last farewell to a friend on the eve of his execution.[5]

It was a matter of only moments for the Earl to slip on the women's dresses and other garments and add false ringlets to his hair. Winifred then painted his face white and applied rouge to his cheeks, in order to hide the long beard that he had grown in captivity.

Then, together with what was seemingly a still hugely upset Mrs Mills, two women left the Tower. One, of course, was Mrs Mills, the other being the Earl dressed as his wife. He went first, holding a kerchief to his face and hiding his distinctly male stature by stooping and stumbling along in front of the crying Mrs Mills. The guards did not look too closely at the 'woman' they had all admired but bowed their heads in respect. Outside, the ever-faithful Cecilia was waiting to escort the Earl back to the lodging house in Drury Lane.

Winifred, Lady Nithsdale, was not finished, however, the plan still had one more phase to complete. Still in her husband's cell, she began what was probably the most dramatic and effective part of the whole affair:

> When I was in the room, I talked to him as if he had really been present, and answered my own questions in my Lord's voice, as nearly as I could imitate it. I walked up and down as if we were conversing together untill I thought they (the escaped prisoner and the women) had time enough to clear themselves of the guards.[6]

Lady Nithsdale then left the Tower, shouting into the guard room and imploring the jailers not to disturb her husband who was, she said 'at his prayers'. Unchallenged, she walked out of the Tower of London, one of only a handful of individuals ever to have hatched and implemented an escape from Britain's most famous prison.

Winifred's last comments on what had been a brave and ingenious escape plan are worth recording. Free from the Tower, the pair first took refuge in Mrs Mills' house, the lodging that could only ever be a temporary respite:

> She had but one small room up the stairs and a very small bed. We threw ourselves upon the bed ... She left us a bottle of wine and some bread, and brought us more in her pocket next day. We subsisted on this provision from Thursday to Saturday night when Mrs Mills came and conducted my Lord to the Venetian ambassador.[7]

After some time in the home of the ambassador, William Maxwell, 5th Earl of Nithsdale, escaped to France dressed as one of the Venetian ambassador's coachmen.

Winifred, who had masterminded the escape, followed him a few weeks later, having gone back to Scotland to ensure that the succession of her eldest son to the title and family estates was in order. She and William lived out the rest of their lives as exiles at the court of the Old Pretender in Rome.

Winifred was undoubtedly a Jacobite hero, someone who fully deserves the acclaim lavished on her for her bravery and cunning. It was an audacious plan, a tribute to love and longing from a member of what were then still called 'the weaker sex'.

However, the other women involved in the escape plan also deserve more recognition than they are usually given. Often overlooked, Cecilia Evans, Mrs Mills and Mrs Morgan/Hiller – all of whom risked capture, prison and maybe even execution – are also worthy of equal credit. They, like Lady Nithsdale, were true Jacobite heroes.

* * *

Isabel Seton, the Countess of Perth was another Jacobite woman who won renown during the '15 Rising. Unlike Lady Nithsdale, however, her fame rests with just one deed.

Isabel Seton, like her husband James, Earl of Perth, was a confirmed Jacobite. He was attainted due to his support of the '15 Rising, losing all of his titles apart from those granted to him by the Jacobites, titles which the Hanoverians did not recognise anyway.

In the wake of the Jacobite defeat in 1715, government troops began to stream northwards to pillage and destroy what they felt were the last vestiges of Jacobitism. The town of Perth had been the scene of one of the few Jacobite successes during the '15 and dislike of the Hanoverian monarchy remained strong in the area. Everyone was expecting trouble.

The Countess of Perth had been disappointed by the result of the recent war but now she was faced by the government forces advancing on her own Concraig Castle. Realising that she had little hope of withstanding a siege, the Countess took what she considered to be her only option. Rather than see the castle captured by the enemy she deliberately set fire to it. The fire took hold and within a few hours, the stronghold was burned to the ground.

Burning Concraig Castle was a selfless act of nationalism by the Countess of Perth, one that ensured her a place in Scottish history. But if the Countess of Perth owes her reputation to just one act, others like Margaret Nairne spent their whole lives supporting the Jacobite cause.

Margaret Nairne, the 2nd Lady Nairne, was a confirmed Jacobite whose support for the exiled king and his descendants lasted from the beginning to the end of the Jacobite period. Born in 1689, one year after the Glorious Revolution, she was the only child of Robert, Lord Nairne. When her father died in 1683, she automatically became Margaret, Baroness of Nairne, a title she held single-handedly for seven years.

She was originally betrothed to Lord George Murray but the engagement was nullified due to his poor health. Instead, in 1690 she married George's brother William. By the marriage William became the 2nd Lord Nairne, eventually being elevated to the rank and title of Earl.

Margaret and her husband had twelve children, all but one of them following in their parents' footsteps and becoming firm Jacobites. One son, Robert, later died at the Battle of Culloden, fighting for Bonnie Prince Charlie.

When the 1715 revolt broke out William immediately joined the Jacobite army. Commander of the second line of Jacobite infantry, he and his son John were captured in the defeat at Preston in November 1715. Found guilty of treason William was sent to the Tower to await execution; John, being of lesser importance, went to Newgate Prison.

Margaret, like her compatriot Lady Nithsdale, was determined to free her husband and son. She travelled to London and began to plead and advocate with government representatives for their reprieve and release.

It took her a while, Margaret even moving in to live with William in the Tower for a large part of the time, but eventually, in August 1517, both father and son were released. Without the unfailing efforts of Margaret Nairne, the reprieve would almost certainly never have happened.

After her husband's release, Margaret retired to her home at Nairne House. Her Jacobite values and beliefs remained firm, however, even when she was forced to spend time re-building the house after the place was accidentally destroyed by fire. The new building supposedly had a window for every day of the year, a phenomenally expensive luxury, but one which appealed to the Young Pretender when Margaret entertained him there during the '45 Rebellion.

Described by later writers as being 'bright among the honoured names of those women who took part in the troubles of their country', Margaret Nairne was one of those people you either loved or hated. The Earl of Mar, defeated general in the '15 Rising, went on record, saying that he wished all of his soldiers had the spirit and the courage as Lady Nairne.

Despite their familial relationship, the Duke of Athol, brother-in-law to Margaret, certainly sat in the latter group. And he was not worried about making public his views on his sister-in-law.

He wrote to his son James, warning the young man about the influence and powers of persuasion Margaret held. It seemed to work as James was the only one of the Duke's four sons to remain loyal to the Hanoverian regime:

> I hope you have as little to do with my Lady Nairne as possible for there cannot be a worse woman. I impute the ruin of my three sons to her artifice.[8]

Whether she was the cause of ruin to Athol's sons or not, Margaret Nairne was genuine and determined in her beliefs. As old age and infirmity set in she found herself not as active as she would have liked. Her passion for the Jacobite cause and love for Bonnie Prince Charlie in particular did not die and she turned to poetry in order to express herself.

Margaret Nairne's most famous poem, the first verse of which was set to music by her grandchild Carolina Oliphant, was a lament for Charles Edward Stuart and his failed hopes in the 1745 Rebellion:

> Bonnie Charlie's noo awa
> Safely o'er the friendly main;
> He'rts will a'most break in twa
> Should he no' come back again.
> (Margaret Nairne and Carolina Oliphant)

Margaret Nairne died in November 1747, just eighteen months after her hopes of seeing Charles Edward Stuart claim the throne had been dashed at Culloden. To the end of her long life, she remained hugely influential on those around her, Jacobite through and through.

* * *

The Jacobite period at the beginning of the eighteenth century coincided with the sudden and dramatic rise of the weekly or monthly journal – magazines by any other name. Joseph Addison and Richard Steele began the process by publishing *The Spectator* and *The Tatler*, journals that were both Whig and firmly Hanoverian in their guiding principles. They were followed, a dozen or so years later, by Henry Fielding's short-lived *The Jacobite Journal*, a decidedly satirical effort published three times a week and designed to humiliate the Jacobites through laughter.

Henry Fielding, one of England's most renowned early novelists, had no time for the Jacobite cause and his editorials were laced with attempts to humiliate not just the male rebels but their female counterparts as well. His spleen continued even after the defeat at Culloden when he complained of Jacobite women dressing up in tartan, even down to the wearing tartan boots:

> The men are going to be joined by "a considerable body of Amazons in plaid jackets, every one of whom is able to fight, aye, and to drink too, without any he-Whig in the Kingdom."[9]

On the other edge of the political spectrum, between 1715 and 1717 George Flint and Isaac Dalton produced a series of what were soon being viewed as treasonable Jacobite journals.

The content of the journals was vitriolic, capturing the anti-government stance of the writers and publishers. The papers were eagerly snapped up by both Tories and, strange as it may seem, by Whigs as well. Flint was the main writer and publisher, Dalton the printer, although both of them doubled up on the others tasks when time and occasion demanded it.

Their most distinctive and popular early journal was the curiously named *Weekly and Political Reflections, Upon the Most Material News Foreign and Domestic*. It was scurrilous and challenging of authority and its contents resulted in George Flint spending several months in Newgate Prison charged with seditious libel. Even from prison, Flint continued to write and publish.

Various name changes saw the journal published in several different guises – as *Robin's Last Shift, The Shift Shifted and The Shift's Last Shift*, the last two appearing in 1717. A cross between academic euphoria, satirical humour and schoolboy enthusiasm, each one gave the critical audience exactly what it needed.

The printer Dalton was also charged and imprisoned with sedition, in his case on four separate occasions. Like Flint, he had a way with words and was able to conjure emotions such as pathos and satirical humour that appealed to all ranks in society. Imprisonment was expected and it was irksome for both men. But that was where a pair of unusual Jacobite women came in.

When Dalton was sentenced to a day in the pillory for his criticism of government policy following the '15 Rising, George Flint was quick to offer support. Rather than just lament the humiliation of Isaac Dalton he seized on the part played by his own wife, in getting *The Weekly Review* out to the public:

> Yet his wife for endeavouring to help her husband (which most think to be a Wife's Duty) and in a way which she could not think unlawful, is also close imprisoned and cannot be let out on Bail, tho' the husband offers to take upon himself whatsoever his Wife can be charged with. Now, one would think her crime could be no less than High Treason and at the same time it is alleged to be no more than ordering the Carriage of a few Newspapers.[10]

To some extent Flint was right but he was also being more than a little disingenuous. On the one hand, his wife's offence could easily be looked on merely as 'carrying newspapers', even if they were considered seditious, if not treasonable. It was not, however, just a bundle of half a dozen papers tied together that she was carrying. She was transporting a great number of them, the content of each one being eagerly awaited by the public.

And Flint was also being less than honest with the truth, as might be expected in the circumstances. With her husband kicking his heels in Newgate, Mrs Flint had not sat idly by but had taken an active role in seeing the journal through the press.

Hardly a Jacobite in the traditional sense, Mrs Flint was bound to fall under the influence of her husband but she was probably more anti-Hanoverian than she was pro-Jacobite. Nevertheless, she managed to do more to keep the journals alive and kicking in their moment of need than many other acknowledged supporters of the Jacobite cause.

She was not alone. It was not long before the Hanoverian finger of justice also began to point in the direction of Isaac Dalton's family.

On 18 August 1717, *The Shift Shifted* led with the otherwise unremarked arrest of Dalton's young sister Mary.

Written by Dalton himself, it began by declaring that he and Flint had undergone much evil for endeavouring to do good for their country. The arrest of Mary Dalton was just one step too far:

> To imprison a man for a Fancy, tho' he be thereby ruin'd, we wave that as a Trifle ... But to take his young Maiden Sister only for happening to receive a little money for him, for this I say, to cram her into a Messenger's and thence bring her to the Bar, all overwhelmed with tears and Confusion, without a moment's Preparation for her Tryal, and thereafter a Fine of 30 Marks, appoint the beautiful young Maiden to remain confined for a Twelve month in a loathsome Gaol, conversing with the Strums of Newgate ... Was ever such a virgin ever so unmercifully expos'd for such a crime.[11]

Dalton's words, each carefully considered before being used, immediately gained sympathy and approval for his sister Mary. Presented to the public as a sentimental heroine who needed to be rescued from the tyranny of government clutches, the piece is almost a forerunner of the later romantic heroines of Scott and Stevenson. It is Jacobite propaganda at its best.

And it worked. When Dalton was later sent to the pillory for his day of humiliation, the crowd cheered him. There was no abuse, no hurling of mud or bad fruit and the other normal greetings for prisoners, only clapping and cries of encouragement. In the wake of the pillory the popularity of Flint, Dawson and their journals escalated sharply, proof positive that it was not just the Jacobites who could make poor, mistaken or unpopular decisions.

The plight of the two women did not help the government in any way. It served only to bring the attention of the public to the need for a free press and, perhaps more than anything, a degree more freedom of speech. Contrary to all expectations, in the wake of their imprisonment, support for Jacobitism soared.

The two women may not have followed the Jacobite armies across heather-filled hills or tended to wounds on the battlefield but Mrs Flint and Miss Mary Dawson were most certainly Jacobite women of the first order.

Chapter Six

Try, Try, Try Again – and an Unexpected Jacobite Heroine

The next potential Jacobite incursion into Britain took place four years after the '15 and was instigated by Guido Alberoni, Chief Minister of Spain. It was to be the only time that Spain became involved in the Jacobite risings.

Plans for the invasion began to be laid as early as the start of 1718 but it was a year later that they finally reached some sort of fulfilment. In a similar way to the long-standing French involvement – now put on the back burner – the Spanish also had an ulterior motive behind their part in this particular invasion scheme. As might be supposed, it had little to do with installing James III, the Old Pretender, on the throne of England.

By the end of 1718, Spain was at war with Britain and other European nations, the War of the Quadruple Alliance as it was called. They had recently lost territory in the Mediterranean and Alberoni's scheme was simple. A Spanish-backed Jacobite invasion of Britain would pull enemy forces away from the Mediterranean, thus giving Spain the opportunity to regain some of the land so recently lost, along with territories taken from them at the end of the War of the Spanish Succession.

In many respects the plan, along with the motivations behind it, was a familiar one. With some modifications, it was little more than a regurgitation of the earlier, French-backed assault of 1715. The fact that the plan had failed before was conveniently forgotten.

A large force of Spanish troops, it was intended, would land in the West Country at the same time as a subsidiary rising took place in Scotland. This Scottish invasion would be backed and led by Charles XII of Sweden whose country was also at odds with Britain. Scottish Jacobites would rise and capture the town and port of Inverness in order to facilitate the Swedish landings from the sea.

The Stuarts must go down as the unluckiest dynasty in the history of the modern world as even before the expeditions got under way things began to go seriously wrong. In December 1718, almost on the eve of the invasion, Charles XII of Sweden died. Without Charles, there would be no Swedish forces and, therefore, no Swedish invasion. And that, of course, left the Scottish rising without any sense of purpose or rationale.

However, King Philip V of Spain was not prepared to leave it there. He had already promised James a fleet of transports along with a number of escort vessels for his proposed landing in the West Country and now, at the urging of Guido Alberoni, things were developed a little further. It was, Philip and Alberoni argued, still a feasible plan; don't delay, launch the attack.

The invasion force consisted of over 5000 experienced and battle-hardened Spanish troops, led by the Jacobite Duke of Ormonde. With his dreams of victory still intact, the Old Pretender could not refuse Philip's offer and despite the death of Charles XII and the abandonment of the Scottish part of the plan, early in March 1719, the Jacobite fleet duly set sail. James would join them once the invasion was successfully driven home.

Disaster struck almost immediately. In the Bay of Biscay, they ran into one of the worst gales in living memory. The ships were scattered, several seriously damaged or were last seen taking flight for the safety of Cadiz Harbour. The Duke of Ormonde had no choice but to return to Spain.

It was not quite all over, however. Later that same month a small force of 300 Spanish soldiers, originally intended to be part of the Jacobite-Swedish incursion, landed at Stornoway on the island of Lewis. There they linked up with 700 Highlanders who had risen in support. Only when they came ashore did the Spanish learn of the disaster that had befallen the main invasion fleet.

Despite this setback, the combined Spanish and Scottish force resolved to fight it out with the government troops. They had some success, taking Eilean Donan Castle, which they managed to hold for some months before government redcoats, aided by a naval bombardment, finally reclaimed it.

The invasion, however, was a pointless exercise with the Jacobite force seemingly having no hope of taking Inverness, the aim of the Jacobite leaders. Ultimately, the ending was a foregone conclusion. Government troops left Inverary on 5 June, sailed to Lewis and established a camp just eight miles away from the Jacobite forces. Eilean Donan Castle, now quartered by just 40 Spanish Marines, surrendered after a brief bombardment from British frigates that had anchored in the loch. The castle was then decimated, using Jacobite gunpowder found in its vaults.

The rebels, under the command of George Keith, were outnumbered but determined to make a good showing. They drew up in defensive formation across the width of Glen Shiel with the Spanish troops in the centre, behind hastily built defensive walls. The Scottish clansmen were situated on their flanks.

The government forces were equipped with portable coehorn mortars that were now being used for the first time in Britain. Firing shells that would burst in the air above the target, showering men with shrapnel, they proved to be far too powerful for the invaders. On 19 June, in a combat which lasted until nine at night, the government troops defeated the combined Jacobite and Spanish forces in what became known as the Battle of Glen Shiel.

There were many distinguished Jacobites present at the battle. The legendary Rob Roy Macgregor and one of his sons were there along with 80 of their clansmen. Cameron of Lochiel and Lord George Murray, later to command Bonnie Prince Charlie's forces during the invasion of 1745, were also significant participants. But the most useful contributor to the Jacobite force was Mackenzie of Seaforth who arrived with 500 Highlanders. It was a welcome addition, even though it was, eventually, help for a lost cause.

Seeing that the day was lost, most of the Jacobites who fought at Glen Shiel, including Rob Roy, managed to slip away in the smoke and confusion caused by the cannonades. They were further aided by the smoke and flames caused when the hillside heather caught fire in the bombardment. The Spanish troops, as they belonged to a formal foreign army, were expatriated back to Spain after surrendering and spending a few months in captivity.

The next few years were depressing for the Jacobites. Several notable exiles like Henry Bolingbroke, the Pretender's foreign minister, and the Earl of Seaforth accepted pardons from the British government and returned home. Active Jacobites like George Keith who had led the Scottish army at Glen Shiel abandoned the cause and went off to fight for the Prussian army. Even James, the Old Pretender, began to think that the game was up.

The death of Louis XIV in 1715 had been a bitter blow for James, particularly following his failed invasion plan from the same year. It was not just friendship and kinship that had suddenly been removed by the death of Louis. The Treaty of Utrecht literally outlawed the Jacobites from France and since then James and his court had been 'treading water', trying to find a home that would match the Chateau de Saint-Germain-en-Laye, their palace outside Paris.

Following the failure at Glen Shiel and to the surprise of everyone, the Pretender suddenly announced that he was about to be married. James had been engaged several times but for one reason or another, he had always failed to follow through. This time his proposed bride was the rich Polish Princess Maria Clementina Sobieska, granddaughter of the Polish King John III. She was to become the most unexpected of all the Jacobite women, rarely praised but far more influential than history has portrayed her.

* * *

The Hanoverian King George I was, naturally, perturbed by the prospect of a match between the Pretender and Princess Clementina. She always preferred her second name to her first, finding it more elegant and socially fitting for a Princess of the royal blood. While that may give some indication of her character, George didn't care what she called herself. She was a threat, that was all he knew and worried about.

If James and Clementina were to have a son then the Jacobite cause would not wither away, as George and most Hanoverian supporters hoped and even expected, but would continue to exist, maybe even grow in strength. Nobody knew what might happen in future years.

George made no secret of his feelings, happily letting it be known that he and the British system of monarchy and government, new as they might be, were diametrically opposed to anything James Stuart might be inclined to do. In particular, anything that might in any way interfere with the succession was taboo.

As a result, Charles VI, the Holy Roman Emperor and a maternal cousin of Clementina, decided it would be politic to placate the English king. The Holy Roman Emperor was arguably the most significant monarch in Europe but there were still limits to his power. Charles could not get to James but he knew that Clementina was within his grasp.

Consequently, Charles had her taken prisoner while she was on her way to Italy for the wedding. He then detained her at Innsbruck Castle. It was a high-handed, not to say dangerous, thing to do. Security was lax, however, and Clementina viewing her imprisonment as an occupational hazard was not prepared to suffer it for any great length of time. It was not long before she managed to affect a rescue and escape from Innsbruck and from the clutches of Charles VI.

James was then in Spain where he had gone to facilitate the planned 1719 invasion of England's West Country and Clementina found it almost impossible to get through enemy territory to meet her bridegroom. They were therefore married by proxy, Clementina's father commenting that his daughter needed to give as much support as possible to her husband. She ought, he said 'to follow his fortune and his cause.'[1]

Clementina took her father's advice. She and James were formally married in Italy on 3 September 1719 and, from the beginning of their turbulent relationship, she did all she could to help and advance the Jacobite cause.

On behalf of her husband James – whom she rather disliked because of his unappealing looks and personality – Clementina did manage to charm the Pope, Clement XI. She was a beautiful woman, a staunch Catholic whose beliefs were later to border on religious mania. As far as the Pope was concerned, she was someone who now had a clear mission in life, even if she did not particularly care for her new partner. She was, Clement decided, exactly what the Pretender needed and duly acknowledged the newly married pair as King and Queen of England, Scotland and Ireland.

Clementina has been criticised by some historians as a woman whose fears and concerns grew into paranoia, something which then adversely affected the personality of James. He certainly developed negative personality traits which manifested themselves in an inability to make important decisions. That failing was perhaps his greatest and gravest fault.

Those negative traits, however, had been present in his personality long before Clementina came into his life. With advancing age, they undoubtedly increased but it is unfair to attribute the blame for the Pretender's depressions and other illnesses on his wife, particularly when there was so much else going wrong with his life.

In addition to regular bouts of depression, James suffered from attacks of quartan fever, a form of malaria where the worst elements of the ague were likely to re-occur every fourth day. There was more. During his life in exile, at one time or another – usually when there was a crisis in his affairs or serious decisions to be made – he went down with illnesses like pneumonia, measles and smallpox. The last rites were wrongly administered to him on no less than three separate occasions.

A poor married relationship might well have made James unhappy but it was unlikely to have turned him into the introverted and inept character that he eventually became. Those traits would have been present since childhood and that leaves Clementina in a position where she was more of a help than a hindrance.

James II, father of the Old Pretender and the original 'Jacobite', had created a Jacobite 'shadow royal court' after the Glorious Revolution of 1688 saw him exiled in France. In many respects, it was a hollow gesture but it did contribute to the process of keeping the Jacobite cause afloat. Willing exiles regularly joined the royal party and visitors were welcomed with all the pomp and grandeur you would expect from a ruling monarch. Recognition from people like The Sun King gave the court exactly the sense of officialdom it required.

When, after the death of Louis XIV and the signing of the Treaty of Utrecht, the Jacobites were obliged to leave France it left them adrift in a very hostile world. Therefore, acceptance by the head of the Catholic Church offered them a very welcome respite.

The Pope's acknowledgement was, in many respects, a mere paper exercise but it did give a degree of credibility and recognition for Clementina's husband. To be named by the Catholic Church as James III of England and James VIII of Scotland was an important gesture, as significant as the earlier recognition by The Sun King. More than anything else, it was a huge boost to the Jacobite cause when things had seemed to be sliding slowly into oblivion.

It is more than likely that without Clementina's presence at James' side, the Papal acknowledgement might never have happened. Unprepossessing, lacking in manners and dignity, having little idea how to deal with people, James was everything his future son, Bonnie Prince Charlie, was not. From the beginning, Clementina knew that she would have to 'fill in the blanks' where her husband was concerned. And with the Pope, she certainly did just that.

James and Clementina lived in some style, thanks to Pope Clement who invited them to reside in Rome at the Palazzo Muti. He granted them an annual allowance and even provided a country villa for their use. Papal guards were appointed to patrol their residence and ensure their safety.

Such comfort and magnificence were essential if the Jacobite leader and exiled monarch was to retain his position and status as the titular head of the English state. It gave him a degree of credibility which, following the dismissal of the Jacobites from France, had seemed to be out of reach for the exiled James. The contribution of Maria Clementina Sobieska in achieving such a success should never be undervalued.

Perhaps one of Clementina's most important contributions to the Jacobite cause, however, was to give birth to a son, Charles Edward Stuart, at the end of December 1720. The famous Bonnie Prince Charlie grew into a significant and hugely popular figure, giving new life and vitality to the Jacobite cause. Despite childhood ailments such as rickets, in keeping with the lives of the illness-prone Stuarts, Charles gradually developed into a handsome and impressive young man.

Without Charles Edward Stuart and, to a much lesser extent, his brother Henry Benedict, Jacobitism might well have ceased to exist after the death of James III in 1766. Even before that date Charles had taken over at the helm of the party, leading the Jacobites in the rebellion of 1745.

As the Papally-recognised Queen of England, Clementina performed many ceremonial duties for the Jacobites. In June 1729, for example, she organised an audience for the Baron de la Brede et la Montesquieu, the renowned philosopher and statesman usually referred to simply as Montesquieu. Amongst many other things, Montesquieu wrote on the need for free-standing independent nations, something dear to Jacobite hearts. The audience with the Pope was a significant achievement for the Jacobite monarchs in exile, Clementina in particular.

After a while, however, the royal marriage dissolved into one of turbulence and general unhappiness. Amongst other complaints, Clementina suspected her husband of having an affair with Marjorie, the wife of James' favourite courtier John Hay. In 1725 she left James and moved into the Ursuline Convent in Rome but still maintained her position and carried out her role as his Queen.

Always close to her eldest son Charles, Clementina did not have such a relationship with Henry who preferred his forthcoming status as Cardinal to the nebulous position of 'King in Waiting'. For James, she had a strange degree of love and dislike. She knew his weaknesses and was careful to boost and develop the personality of Charles, her son. Perhaps too much so, as his later career would show.

Clementina was eventually reconciled with her husband and had John and Marjorie Hays dismissed from his court. But despite this seeming success, she still spent most of her remaining years living apart from James. When she died of scurvy in 1736, the new Pope Clement XII ordered that she be given a state funeral. Such was the significance of Maria Clementina Sobieska, the largely unrecognised but crucially important Jacobite Queen in exile.

* * *

If Clementina and James represented the glittering upper crust of the Jacobite movement, there were several other layers below them.

The Jacobite Societies and Clubs, so redolent of the period, catered for the mid-range of individuals, the Squires and land owners of England and Wales. Their behaviours and attitudes brought them scorn and approbation from the Whig writers and satirists of the eighteenth and nineteenth centuries.

Henry Fielding, a fervent Whig supporter and one of the early British proponents of the novel as an art form, was probably the most renowned of these writers. Although his earlier books, *Tom Jones* and the like, were more comedic and theatrical in design, he was not above spreading fears of murdering and raping Tory Jacobites. Of course, such atrocities never materialised but as he grew older and more successful, Fielding came to view the novel as a tool with which to batter opponents and members of the various Jacobite societies:

> He was by birth, education and literary sympathies much more closely allied with the earlier eighteenth-century groupings that despised novels than with the classes for which they were the chief reading matter.[2]

Bloated and self-indulgent seems to have been the general opinion regarding Tory supporters, albeit a judgement made largely in hindsight and fuelled by nothing more than rumour. Historian and poet Lord Macauley produced a stereotypical portrait of what he thought a typical Jacobite Society member would be like – 'a bigoted, ignorant, drunken philistine'.[3]

In some respects, Macauley was perfectly correct but, of course, the same description could be given to many of the Whig supporters of the government and of Hanoverian society in general, including Macauley himself. Even so, the description has become something of an accepted fact, almost a cliché. Macauley would be proud of the accomplishment.

The chiefs or leaders of the Scottish clans provided another level. Different from the members of the English Jacobite Societies, the clan chiefs ruled their people in a traditional patrician way. It was a hierarchical society, one geared for war, but more than anything else its values meant that those at the top of the social and economic tree had a duty to protect and ensure that those beneath them were provided with suitable levels and standards of living. If that duty was missing then rebellion and riot were the natural order of things.

It was a sense of duty that went both up and down, the same sense of purpose being apparent in the attitudes of the clan chiefs to the deposed King and his descendants. The King was the one person who did not owe fidelity to any living being, only to God. Therefore, to replace one king with another without the blessing of God and to then proclaim loyalty to the new monarchy was not acceptable. Reinforced by Catholic and Episcopalian beliefs, it soon became obvious where the loyalty of the clan chiefs, and therefore of the clansmen, truly lay.

The clan chiefs were not above displays of self-interest, however. Many of them deliberately stood apart from any rising, sending their sons to fight for the Jacobite cause but not actually engaging in rebellion themselves. That way, they could still claim the glory of victory but if defeat should occur the chiefs could always state that their orders not to fight for the Jacobite cause had been disobeyed by their sons and by the clansmen.

The final group comprised the coal-face exponents of the various rebellions, the ordinary working men and women of Britain. Labourers, shop keepers, itinerant salesmen, small subsistence farmers, coal miners and so on were hardly the most vocal of Jacobite supporters but they were the ones who would stand, unflinching, in the battle lines when the time came.

Just as there were Jacobite societies, the ordinary Jacobite supporters soon found themselves centres where they could relax and feel at home:

> Everywhere there were substantial numbers of Jacobites there were bound to be Jacobite ale houses, inns and taverns.

Whether they were run by sympathetic landlords or simply businessmen with an eye to the main chance, most plebian Jacobites as a result had a 'social space' that was peculiarly their own. There they could fraternise with people of like mind, sing seditious songs, tell salacious stories about the Hanoverians, give money to sustain Jacobite prisoners, and even on occasions be recruited for Jacobite risings.[4]

The government occasionally went as far as to close down the most riotous of these drinking dens but that invariably resulted in further riot and public disturbance. And, of course, with one ale house closed to them the Jacobite men could simply choose another to make their own. Much better to play a 'hidden' game and support gangs of thugs to smash up the centres of Jacobite leisure activity. With the succession of the Hanoverians the employment of the various groups of ruffians, aimed at meeting and defeating the Tory-run Jacobite street gangs, became fairly common place in London.

The Whig/government groups were named Mug-house gangs, after the original Mug House Club in Long Acre, a non-violent middle class drinking club that had been founded as a way of keeping up the Protestant succession after the death of Queen Anne and the accession of George I. Daniel Defoe wrote that you had to be in the club 'by seven to get Room, and after ten the Company are for the most part gone'.[5] The new Mug-house gangs, however, were the direct opposite. For them violence was natural and a reason for existence.

By the 1720s there were many government-sponsored groups based in drinking dens across London. They waged a virtually incessant war against similar Jacobite groups, conflicts that regularly saw broken bodies and destroyed buildings.

Eventually, after one death too many in one of the brawls, the government forced legislation through Parliament, hanged several members of various groups and even went as far as destroying or pulling down many of the ale houses.[6] It brought the Mug-house era to an end.

Yet again, there appears to have been little or no female activity in the Mug-house wars, from either side of the conflict. Yet it remains difficult to imagine the rioters in action without encouragement from their female counterparts. Supposition, yes; fact, possibly.

Try, Try, Try Again – and an Unexpected Jacobite Heroine

The Mug-house riots in London might, then, be a little hazy as far as female participation is concerned. At the other end of the spectrum, what we do know is that dozens of women followed the Jacobite armies at various times. They were wives, sisters, even daughters of the Jacobite soldiers. Some were undoubtedly prostitutes and many brought their children with them when they marched off to war alongside the soldiers. But, at the end of the day, the sex of the camp followers was immaterial; they were there to support their menfolk and to use a later phrase or description, they were there to 'do their bit'!

There may well have been illicit relationships between the soldiers and the women, certainly the unwedded ones. It would have been unnatural to do otherwise as close contact between the sexes in times of crisis was a breeding ground for deep feelings and longings. But with relationships between men and women so free and pleasant, there was little unwanted and unnecessary attention, no violent assaults or rapes. In fact, instances of violent sexual crime were virtually non-existent. Men and women existed happily together in the camps and on the march.

As Maggie Craig has written, the '45 was a civil war with whole towns and villages divided by their choice of faction. The Jacobite cause, no less than support for the Hanoverian monarchy, was capable of splitting families apart and almost to the last minute nobody really knew the direction which the emotions might take or the strength of feeling in family and friends.[7]

All of which meant that many of the married women in the Jacobite camps felt they had no choice but to accompany their men. The fear of being locked out, rejected and spurned by families who had given their support to the Hanoverians, was too great. Being on the tramp with their husbands might have been physically dangerous but it was also morally quite sound.

* * *

One of the more unpleasant results of risings like the '15 was the decision to use transportation, not just for criminals like thieves, robbers and the like but for dozens of Jacobite supporters. In the eyes of the government, of course, Jacobite supporters *were* actually criminals, even the women and children who may or may not have been involved in any of the risings.

The intention of transportation was three-fold. One, to cripple the Catholic community of Britain; two, to put fear into the minds of rank-and-file rebels as a means of punishment; and three, of encouraging petitions from people of position, thus showing that the Whig monarchy and government could offer retribution tinged with clemency.[8]

In reality, clemency was never on the cards. The process of transportation meant that entire families – men, women and children regardless of age or health – were ripped out from their homes and sent off to the Americas and to West Indian Islands. Execution of significant rebels still took place but this was another, more subtle version of punishment.

Deportation or transportation began in 1716, just a few months after the '15 rising. Ten ships were filled with Jacobites, the total of prisoners numbering just over 1300, and despatched to Virginia and Maryland. In all, Jacobite prisoners were sent to nine different American settlements, or states as they were soon to become, where many of them were treated like slaves. Many more settled down and made the USA their home.

The same month that the first Jacobite ships left for the Americas a further eight vessels, with slightly fewer prisoners on board, headed for West Indian islands like Barbados and Antigua. There the heat and disease soon killed off many of the more helpless or infirm Jacobite families in a delayed, different but highly effective programme of capital punishment.

Estimates for the total number of Jacobites sent to foreign parts vary greatly. Many of the lists detailing the deportees do not give a crime so there is often no way to differentiate between political prisoners and ordinary criminals. The infamous Dr Johnson was clear in his opinions about the quality and value of the convicts in America. Never one to hold back on an idea or notion, he did not differentiate between Jacobites and other criminals and was not afraid to give his opinion, loudly and in public:

> In 1769 Dr Johnson, speaking of the Americas said to a friend "Sir, they are a race of convicts and ought to be content with anything we allow them short of hanging."[9]

It has been estimated that the two major Jacobite risings, 1715 and 1745, saw upwards of 1600 men, women and children being transported across the Atlantic. The figure is a guesstimate, the true and more accurate total is quite likely to be higher.[10]

Transportation was, in many respects, a fore-runner of the infamous clearances that were to follow the '45. It was cruel but it was effective, a way to weed out undesirable elements in society and send them where they could do least damage. That was the government view. The alternative was to clog up the various gaols across Britain, fill them to the brink with women and children, leaving no room for future offenders.

There is little doubt that the government view of the Jacobite women was anything but favourable, particularly towards those women of some standing and leadership in the country. As one anonymous Whig commentator remarked:

> Jacobite women present a threat to humanity because they display a lust for power, cruelty, revenge and all the horrors of destructive war.[11]

The fear of emasculation is clearly apparent in that comment which goes beyond dislike and fear and ends up bordering on misogyny. It is almost worthy of Dr Johnson himself!

Chapter Seven

Jacobite Calling Cards

The long empty gap between the 1719 disaster at Glen Shiel and the arrival in Scotland of the Young Pretender in 1745 was a twenty-six-year period of hiatus for the Jacobites. It was an age – and it did genuinely seem like an age to the waiting Stuart supporters - of no invasions but plenty of thinking; a time of many regrets but no action; a time when opposition to the Hanoverians was limited to poems, songs and Jacobite totems that were seemingly the only way to now declare your loyalty to the exiled Stuart dynasty and the Old Pretender.

It was also a time of spies and undercover agents. The English and Scottish Jacobites had always been convinced that if their aims were to be realised then they would need external support, both financially and militarily, and consequently spent much of the time in the 1720s and 30s approaching foreign powers. The response of the Hanoverian government was to set its spies and agents to uncover potential links and, if necessary, thwart them:

> Thus, the half century of struggle between the rival governments following the failure of the '15 has a Cold War flavour to it ... Jacobite and Hanoverian agents spied on, and occasionally attempted to murder, each other. Letters were intercepted, messengers and trusted confidents suborned.[1]

Inevitably the Hanoverians with their wide range of diplomatic contacts and espionage networks were far better and far more successful at the spying game than their opponents. They were able to cut off potential help for the Jacobites, often before it materialised, one of several reasons why there were no successful landings by opposition forces between 1719 and 1745.

It was not all doom and gloom, however. One of the more successful Jacobite activities during these years was smuggling. Taking place mainly along the south and south east coasts of England, by the early years of the eighteenth-century smuggling had become big business. Tea, brandy, wine, luxury goods that were all liable for excise tax put money into the coffers of individual Jacobite supporters. The extent of profit from smuggled goods was enormous – at one stage a smuggled keg of fine French brandy could make three times its purchase price in England.

But it was not just a financial activity, welcome as this might be for the Jacobites. Perhaps more importantly, the various smuggling gangs provided information on the movements of the Hanoverian forces. It was an invaluable source of material.

The Pretender may have failed in 1715 and 1719, albeit failed from a distance, but support for him and for what was increasingly being viewed as something of a lost cause remained significant. Memories were potent emotions with the result that poetry and songs, mostly sentimental poetry and songs, kept his image alive:

> Sound the shrill trumpet, fill its silver womb
> With sweeter Notes than ever yet were blown
> Great British Majesty to welcome home.
>
> (anonymous)[2]

And so on for another seventeen verses! The above example may be somewhat celebratory, even a little hopeful, predicting the return of a British rather than a German king, but most of the Jacobite airs from this period were mournful and, in an appealing sort of way, quite maudlin. That was perhaps understandable as the songs were supposedly speaking of lost loves and displaying a heart-rending longing for times gone by.

View the ballads and songs of the age as personal laments, if you will; but think of them also as metaphorical comments on a lost dynasty. Almost without fail, the songs catch the sense of emotional dejection that engulfed the Jacobite communities at the time.

The authorship of a large number of Jacobite songs from this period remain anonymous, reflecting safety in secrecy. To declare outright ownership of a song or piece of poetry which was critical of the Hanoverian monarchy was asking for trouble.

That also applied even to the more obscure or obtuse pieces that carried a hidden message, a sidelong glance at 'what might have been' in personal relationships had it not been for some unnamed tragedy. Many failed to realise it but they were also a comment on the political situation and, if the Hanoverian government cared to unravel the metaphors, were potential minefields for the composers. Best, then, to keep all ownership hidden.

Perhaps because of this, the songs were still incredibly popular for years after the Jacobite cause had withered and died. Many are still regarded as old favourites and are still sung today in schools, folk clubs and writing circles:

> By yon bonnie banks and by yon bonnie braes
> Where the sun shines bright on Loch Lomond,
> Where me and my true love were ever wont to gae,
> On the bonnie, bonnie banks of Loch Lomond.
> Oh, ye'll tak the high road and I'll tak the low road
> And I'll be in Scotland afore ye;
> But me and my true love with never meet again
> On the bonnie, bonnie banks of Loch Lomond.
> (Original version anon, circa 1745,
> rewritten circa 1846)[3]

Accompanied by pipes or even sung without the aid of any musical instrument, the emotions and pictures conjured by songs like *The Bonnie Banks of Loch Lomond* (above) were sure to stir the hearts of most Scottish men and women while they were waiting for the next – and surely more successful? – Jacobite incursion. Sung in the quiet of the evening hour or bawled out in the smoke and stench of the traveller's inn, the songs had a power that has been equalled only by the Irish laments of a later age.

Robert Burns, or Robbie Burns as he is invariably called, was Scotland's national poet. He was born some years after the last Jacobite landing, led by the Young Pretender, and while not overtly Jacobite in his outlook he was a Stuart supporter by instinct and strongly opposed to the 1707 union with England.

He was not afraid to lay out his views in his verse. His 1791 poem decrying the union of the two nations is a classic example of his views. And those were not just his views, many Scots born before and after Culloden, felt exactly the same:

> But pith and power, till my last hour
> I'll mak' this declaration,
> We're bought and sold for English gold –
> Such a parcel o' rogues in a nation.'
>
> (Robert Burns)[4]

Sentiment and romanticism apart, there were also many more aggressive or challenging poems written in the security of Jacobite drinking dens and houses. You would have needed a belly full of whiskey or ale to sing the following lyrics out loud. It was first published in 1810 but written sometime in the years before the death of King George I, the *Wee German Lairdie* of the title, in 1727. The exact date is unknown:

> Wha the de'il hae we gotten for a king
> But a wee, wee German Lairdie.
> Wha we gaed to bring him hame
> He was delvin' in his yairdie.
> He was sheughing kail and pu'in leeks,
> Aye but the hose an' but the breeks
> Wi his beggar duds he cleeks
> Ye wee bit German Lairdie.'
>
> (Anon)[5]

The romanticising of the Jacobite period which came later with Sir Walter Scott and others undoubtedly helped to keep the songs of the time alive and well-used. In the wait for the Young Pretender, they were talismans and tokens that every Scot, every Jacobite, could see and understand. More importantly, they were literary items that were pitched directly at them and to which they could all relate.

The surge of poetic enthusiasm did not end with the '45. The defeat at Culloden may have marked the end of a political epoch, the finish of Stuart hopes regarding England's throne, but it did not see the end of what can now be genuinely called a literary movement. The lyrical ballads and laments may not have been perfectly crafted, at least not at first, but they were adapted and edited by later writers and anthologists into the poems that we see and hear today.

The lasting quality of these poems and songs, works that were then and are now, truly poetry of the people, lies in their ability to catch deep feelings and express them in a way that grabs at the heart and soul. They were not, in the main, the product of professional writers but, rather, the work of ordinary men and women.

It took the careful editing and, sometimes, the re-writing of the ballads by men like James Hogg for his 'Jacobite Relics' of 1819 in order to complete their survival. Even in their edited form they are, however, a testament to the ability and to the willingness of those ordinary men and women to express deeply held emotions in verse.

Created, first, in the long 'waiting period' between defeat in 1719 and the even more substantial defeat at the Battle of Culloden in 1746, the Jacobite songs did not die after the movement withered away. As far as poetry and songs were concerned Culloden was not a defeat but a watershed. The renowned poet and critic Hugh MacDiarmid once wrote:

> The splendid renaissance of the Forty-Five had thus culminated in the remarkable result that there was scarcely a parish or a clachan throughout the Highlands and Islands that had not its own poet.[6]

That remains a significant tribute to what were often untrained, uneducated hands. It was People's Poetry of the finest style, holding a power that was probably not equalled until the soldiers' verses from the trenches in the First World War.

Equally as important, a significant number of the poems were written by women. In a patriarchal society, women were still viewed as second-rate citizens by the half-shut eyes of many. Poetry and songs? That was fine, they were needed and were something at which women could excel. Leave the fighting to the men!

It was a blinkered approach; most of the bigoted and opinionated misogynists failed to realise that the tasks they had happily passed down to the women were, in themselves, vehicles for change and development.

Slowly but surely, attitudes were beginning to alter and there is no doubt that the literary quality of women's writing during the Jacobite era had a great deal to do with that change. The strength of the words and the raw power of the imagery of the time is still caught in the emotion that runs through almost every composition.

* * *

If you were a Scot or a confirmed Jacobite it was not just poetry that showed your affiliation during the long waiting time between the battles of Glen Shiel and Culloden. There were a number of talismans or tokens that also demonstrated your support for the Jacobite cause.

The most obvious of these was the tartan. There have been many myths about the origin, use and meaning of tartan and, in particular, the tartan kilt. Spurious or real, it did not stop the Jacobites wearing plaid shawls and kilts in their various campaigns.

The idea that the plaid colours of the kilt represented certain objects and beliefs apparently became popular during the days before the Jacobites but whether or not that belief was genuine is another matter altogether. According to legend the red patterns in a tartan kilt or shawl were there so that blood did not show on the garments while blue represented Scotland's lochs and rivers. Green stood for the forest, yellow for the crops of the country. Red and green also stood for Catholicism, blue for the Protestants.[7]

So, truth or fiction? It does sound rather like the type of legend that story tellers might invent and use to enthral their audience. Or maybe not. If it is not true then perhaps it should be. It is too charming a concept to be mere fiction.

It was not until the middle years of the nineteenth century that tartans became associated with specific clans or families. Clansmen and women had worn tartan kilts, shawls and blankets for many years, the earliest known example of a kilt being the Falkirk Tartan which dates from the third century CE. And in all of their many campaigns Scottish troops had invariably worn kilts into battle. It made their appearance both startling and frightening.

However, the colours and the patterns on the clansmen's kilts during the Jacobite risings were hardly uniform. The choice of colours and styles was up to them. Paintings from the time show regiments of Jacobite Highlanders dressed in kilts with as many as twenty or more different patterns and colours on the cloth.

The association of specific tartans with the concept of 'blood identity' was clearly nowhere near as specific as it later became. It is certainly not fiction but the view that we have of the Highlanders in their clan tartans owes more to writers like Scott and Stephenson than it does to reality. As so often happens in history, fiction bred fact and in this case did it so effectively that the origins of the clan tartans have been misted over or even lost along the way.

It hardly mattered. The sight of the clansmen in their kilts, a multitude of colours and styles, caused more than a little trepidation in the Hanoverian soldiers opposing them in the various risings – even though many of the government troops were actually Scottish. Their leaders marked down the effect for future use. So, too, did the Hanoverian government in London.

The presence of many Scots in the army of Butcher Cumberland and other Hanoverian generals was, in some respects, pragmatism at its height. Soldiering meant security in terms of wages and food, something that was not to be sneered at in difficult economic times. There was some religious tension – Protestant English army against Catholic Jacobites – but not nearly as much as has been supposed. Similarly, inter-clan hostility had something to do with the makeup, as did the old chestnut of Lowlanders versus Highlanders. Ultimately, it was down to a mixture of all the reasons and causes.

In the wake of their crushing victory at Culloden, the government decided it was time to clamp down on anything that even remotely smacked of nationalism. Chief amongst these was the Dress Act of 1746 which banned the wearing of tartan and other items of Gaelic culture.

The ruling was intended to help destroy the Scottish identity but it clearly did not work. The same year that the Dress Act was passed it was estimated that 90% of the women in Edinburgh were still wearing tartan, regardless of the new law.

Only one woman, Jean Rollo, was arrested for wearing tartan. This happened on 20 December, the birthday of the Bonnie Prince Charlie. Brought before Lord Albemarle, Jean Rollo successfully argued her case and was released from custody. Rollo's victory was just the tip of the iceberg. That deliberate 'disobedience' continued, so much so that when the Dress Act was repealed in 1822, the kilt and the tartan were adopted as the national dress of Scotland.

The concept of nationalism became particularly strong in the years following the passing of the Act of Union in 1707. As part of that nationalism the need to belong – to families, to extended families, to villages, to clachans - became hugely important. It was one way of showing unity in the face of oppression and the best way of displaying that unity and need to belong was through the wearing of your clan tartan. There was more.

Jacobite Calling Cards

The multi-coloured kilts and shawls that had been worn in the early days of the Jacobite movement had clearly had their moment. It meant that around the time of the 1715 rising the Jacobites took the idea of the tartan kilt and, moving beyond the simple need to belong, began to think of it as a token or expression of Scottishness.

When the Jacobite tartan pattern was created in Edinburgh in 1713 it became hugely popular and was worn in public by men and by women. That popularity caused the Hanoverian government some concern but the Jacobite supporters felt secure in their choice of dress and in the message, it was giving to the government forces. They could not be prosecuted as, after all, they were only wearing a garment of clothing. It was another thirty years before the Hanoverian government got round to banning the kilt.

King George IV visited Scotland in 1822. He was the first English monarch to formally venture north of the border for nearly 200 years. His visit was hugely significant, a gesture that began, along with the lifting of the Dress Act, a craze for Scottish clothing. George's motivation for wearing the kilt and plaid is not really known – it's effect certainly is.

The novelist and poet Sir Walter Scott took charge of organising the approved festivities around the King's visit and did so with such pomp and glamour that the celebrations were christened 'Sir Walter's Certified Pageantry.' Scott's organisation of the events brought humour to many, un-equalled nationalism for others.[8]

Despite the satirical comment, the activities helped to create a huge interest in Scottish culture and in the popularity of Scottish dress. Such was the explosion of interest in all things Scottish that Sir Walter Scott is, in some quarters, often wrongly credited with inventing the kilt and other aspects of Scottish culture.

* * *

Flowers and plants were highly significant for Jacobite supporters, in particular the white rose. Commonly found growing wild in hedgerows, the Burnet Rose or, to give the flower its correct name, the rosa spinosissma, was both beautiful and available.

A white rose was supposedly plucked from its bush by Bonnie Prince Charlie when he landed in Scotland in 1745 but the flower had been significant for Jacobites long before that. Carrying one or wearing a broach in the shape of the flower were hardly treasonable offences and it was one way of making a point with Hanoverians.

Glass was hugely popular and Jacobite crystal glasses can still be found in circulation at Antique fairs. Their survival remains a little surprising, considering the propensity for toasting 'The King Over the Water' during wild nights of hope and celebration.

Kilt pins, often in the shape of a dagger with an enamel rose on the hilt or handle, were another popular ornamentation. Plaid broaches for women were equally as popular. Originally intended to be a useful way of pinning a shawl or blouse, with obvious Jacobite symbols they quickly became yet another way of defying Hanoverian rules.

The birthday of James III, the old Pretender, was 10 June, always called White Rose Day by the Jacobites, and was a specific day, more than any other in the year, when it was important to wear a white rose of some description. Writing much later, long after the Jacobite rebellions had ended, the poet Hugh MacDiarmid beautifully caught the significance and the power of the tiny flower:

> The rose of all the world is not for me.
> I want for my part
> Only the little white rose of Scotland
> That smells sharp and sweet – and breaks the heart.[9]
>
> (Hugh MacDiarmid)

A flower with one bud was meant to represent Charles Edward Stuart, the Young Pretender. Two buds were for both Charles and his younger brother Henry. A variation of the white rose was the white cockade, worn on a blue bonnet, the two colours sharply defined and visible to everyone. That, perhaps more than anything else, was a statement that Jacobite women in particular took to their hearts.

Other flowers and insects were also symbolic. Sunflowers were considered special as they invariably turned their heads to the sun. That was, in the eyes of the Jacobites, proof of loyalty to, first, the exiled James II, then to the Old Pretender and finally his son. Butterflies and moths were regarded as symbols of re-birth, in this case the re-birth of the Stuart dynasty, while bees represented the loyalty that was so important to the Jacobite cause.

A six-pointed star was said to represent royalty, Stuart royalty of course, while birds such as the jay were thought to be lucky. The letter J started both the name of the bird and the name of James II, the one true king! The wearing of a white waistcoat was also taken to mean the wearer was supporting the Jacobite cause. Quite what that did for the formal attire of fashionable gentlemen remains unclear.

There was more, much more. Acorns and oak leaves, usually shown in drawings or pictures on the walls of ladies' boudoirs, were a popular Stuart symbol. They were meant to commemorate the escape of King Charles II, the Prince of Wales as he then was, from Parliamentary clutches after the Battle of Worcester at the end of the English Civil War. The story of the Prince hiding in the branches of an oak tree had already gone down in folklore; the Jacobite purloining of the myth through veneration of the oak tree was a convenient way of celebrating the Stuart dynasty and showing that support for the exiled royals went beyond the Scottish border.

Jacobite medals, trinket boxes, delicate white china cups and saucers with the picture of a knight or shepherd stencilled onto the sides, dozens of such small items were available. They were innocuous items that could sit easily on a lady's dressing table or sideboard without causing panic or concern in government circles and were avidly collected by women who would not be allowed to go within ten miles of a battlefield.

Jacobite societies continued to be popular. The most famous of these was the Cycle of the White Rose, founded by the Williams-Wynn family from north Wales in 1710. The society or club came to be known as The Cycle Club before being incorporated, in the late Victorian period, into the Order of the White Rose. There were many more similar groups, all over Britain. To some extent it is the Jacobite society meeting that we think of when we try to visualise 'gentlemanly' opposition to the Hanoverian government.

***

We also tend to think of the Jacobite risings as being a specifically Scottish series of rebellions. That, however, was very far from the case.

The English West Country, Cornwall and Devon in particular, were apparently hotbeds of Jacobite fervour although there were few instances of action involving the West Country men and women during the

Jacobite period. The area was a long way from the centre of government and, in the past, had often been the centre for rebellion and riot. It had twice been thought of by the exiled Jacobite monarchs and their foreign allies as an ideal place for a landing and a rising. As it happened, the plans came to nothing.

Ireland, of course, was always a potential danger area for the English crown and government. King William's victory at the Battle of the Boyne in 1689 was a significant setback for the Jacobites but it did not end the Irish resistance. The Williamite War or the War of the Two Kings as it is sometimes known, dragged on for another two years before the Jacobite defeat at the Battle of Aughrim in County Galway on 22 July 1691 brought matters to a close.

The Battle of Aughrim is sometimes referred to as the bloodiest battle ever fought on British soil with approximately 4000 Jacobites and between 1000 and 2000 Williamites killed. Many more were wounded and later died from their injuries. Over 500 Jacobites were taken prisoner.

However, it was the brutality of the after-battle tactics by government forces that horrified supporters of the exiled James. Jacobite bodies were left to rot on the field of battle, some of them lying there for two or three years. Scavenging dogs and birds devoured their flesh until there were only white and glistening bones left to mock the dead.

Women from the nearby village of Aughrim managed to bury some of the slain but there were more bodies than the handful of women could effectively deal with. There were very few men in the village, most of them having left to join the Jacobite forces with the result that everything more or less fell back on the women.

As far as the Williamites were concerned, the bodies were a symbol of defeat for the Jacobite Catholic forces. That was in contrast to the terms of the Treaty of Limerick, signed in October 1691, which formally brought hostilities to a close and gave Catholics the freedom to practice their religion provided they pledged loyalty to William and Mary.

The Treaty of Limerick might have brought open hostilities to an end but it did not halt the Jacobite fervour. Legislation from the English Parliament, acts and bills such as The Disarming Act of 1695, were hardly calculated to annoy the Irish but that is exactly what they did. By the terms of the Disarming Act, no one was allowed to possess a firearm worth more than £5, something that hit not only the Jacobite supporters but farmers, gamekeepers and others who relied on the land for their living.

The Flight of the Wild Geese, as the process became known, was the term used to describe the mass exodus out of Ireland that followed implementation of the Treaty of Limerick. Rather than swear allegiance to England's joint sovereigns, over 20,000 Catholics, men, women and children, immediately left their homeland to take up residence in France.

Over the next ten or twenty years they were joined by many more. To begin with, most of the men became part of James II's 'army in exile.' After his death, the Irish Jacobites were merged with France's Irish Brigade. Others chose to remain in Ireland where they became underground fighters against the Williamite forces. Still more, sensing that Jacobitism was finished, changed sides and enlisted in William's army.

The Battle of Aughrim was, for some time, more celebrated than William's earlier victory on the Boyne. It featured in a play by Robert Aston and was commemorated in a poem by Richard Murphy – who had relatives fighting on both sides in the battle.

Although the Irish Catholics viewed a return by James II and his descendants as the best way of getting their religion back on an approved footing, they failed to join the rising when the Young Pretender landed in Scotland in 1745. That reluctance was partially due to the failure of Jacobite forces to come ashore in significant numbers in Ireland but it was, like so many of the Jacobite enterprises, yet another missed opportunity.

* * *

Links between the Jacobites and the Freemasons have been spoken about for many years. Jacobites certainly saw Freemasonry as a way of helping them to achieve their aims, although it has never been totally clear what form that help might take! On the other extreme, the Hanoverian government felt the secrecy surrounding the masonic movement was threatening the security of the country. Freemasons, in the eyes of many Hanoverians, were simply part of a gigantic Jacobite conspiracy.

The closeness and secrecy of the organisation appealed to the Jacobites but the regular members' meetings were more of an opportunity for political discussion than a clandestine organisation plotting treason and mayhem. The secrecy of the Freemasons and their reliance on ritual merely strove to reinforce the idea of anti-government plots in the minds of those Hanoverian supporters already reeling with paranoia.

Perhaps the greatest gift the Freemasons gave to the Jacobite cause came in their network of Masonic Lodges. Established in many British communities the Lodges were tiny havens of comfort for travelling or itinerant workers. In theory at least, their regular meetings saw offerings of warmth and companionship to fellow masons, regardless of their affiliations and loyalty. Above all, these meetings gave Protestants and Catholics the opportunity to meet on equal terms, meetings that were far more secure than any of the Jacobite societies.[10]

Despite this, there were regular struggles between government and Jacobite influences within the movement, usually based on who would control the meetings and the organisation. The political connections between Jacobites and Freemasons, like serious Jacobitism itself, died out in the years immediately following the defeat at Culloden in 1746. Freemasonry remained a significant force for many more years.

Viewed now, in hindsight, the early eighteenth century was a time of change for women, particularly for Scottish Jacobite women. The beginnings of the later Scottish Enlightenment were there long before Culloden, women starting to realise that there was more to life than marriage, drudgery and compliance to male will. They did not know it at the time but this was the beginning of a significant British cultural revolution.

In the early part of the century, there were no salons in Britain, as there were in France, places where women could go to talk to other women without male interference and gain support and relief. Coffee houses there were, even though by the end of the seventeenth century the craze for coffee had been superseded by a similar desire for tea, but these were almost exclusively the preserve of the male members of society.

However, what women did have available to them were their bedrooms, bedchambers as they were known, and during the period of the great waiting that was where the young middle-class Scottish women met to drink tea, gossip and exchange ideas. As the great wait went on, rumour was running rife and, even before he finally landed in 1745, it was centred on the handsome, tantalising figure of Bonnie Prince Charlie:

> They were talking of little else but the young Prince come to reclaim the throne of his ancestors. Rebellion was in the air – not just against the political status quo, but a social and intellectual rebellion too.[11]

Academics and scholars like Frances Hutcheson and Lord Pitsligo were now writing and talking openly about how women had been undervalued for years. Such academic tomes might not have reached the bothies and the glens of the Sottish clansmen and women but they did hit home in the minds and hearts of the middle- and upper-class Scottish families – and the men and women from these groupings would be the leaders in what was soon to come.

For perhaps the first time in recent history women had suddenly found a degree of freedom of expression that was shocking to their elders and pleasing to men like Hutcheson and Pitsligo. There were no rigid controls, either in speech or in conduct, very different from the codes of conduct women were later to have inflicted on them in the High Victorian period:

> Relations between the sexes were free and easy. Chaperones were a feature of a later age and young men and women, whilst supervised to a certain extent, were allowed to walk, talk and ride out together in comparative freedom.[12]

Small wonder, then, that many of the ballads written in these years came from the pens and souls of women. There were several well-known women poets at this time, most notable being Lady Grizzel Baillie and Lady Elizabeth Wardlaw.

Neither of them were renowned as Jacobites or even on the opposite extreme as Hanoverian supporters although Grizzel Baillie came from a Covenanting family, her father having been suspected of involvement in the Rye House Plot of 1683. Grizzel smuggled food to her father when he was in hiding but that seems to have been the full extent of her involvement in politics.

The family, Grizzel included, sought refuge in Holland until after the Glorious Revolution when they returned to Scotland. Grizzel's full body of work was not published in her lifetime, only appearing in print after her death in 1746.

Elizabeth Wardlaw seems to have had even less involvement than Grizzel Baillie with the underground world of Hanoverian politics. Her claim to fame lies in the *Ballad of Hardyknute*, published in 1718 but thought by many to be simply an old poem that she had discovered and adapted, and in the *Ballad of Sir Patrick Spens*.

The importance of the two women is simply that they were poets, writing and publishing in an age dominated by men and in a profession that had always been regarded as a male preserve. They were the tip of a very large underground movement, a rumbling volcano waiting to explode.

This was a time when the identity of Scotland became defined by one word – resistance. That meant resistance to the one great power that now had taken on a role of distinct menace. Scotland had faced such a prospect many times before, notably in the days of William Wallace and Robert the Bruce, but now the threat was significantly stronger and the chances of surviving it greatly lessened by the events of the previous few decades.

Real-life bandits like Rob Roy MacGregor assumed a significance they had never held before. In Rob Roy's case, he became a national figure through breaking the law as somebody who had been wronged by authority and was seeking revenge. He was not, at least in the eyes of the Scots, seen as an outlaw intent on wronging others for personal gain.

By the 1720s much of the drive behind resistance was centred not so much on restoring the Stuart monarchy as on the desire to destroy the 1707 Act of Union with England:

> Why did You thy Union break
> Thou had of late with France?[13]

France had traditionally been the other party to stand alongside Scotland in the 'Auld Alliance,' each country vowing to come to the others aid should England threaten. That, after the Treaty of Utrecht, was no longer the case. New alliances would have to be forged, notably with Spain.

In the meantime, the unique heritage and identity of Scotland would have to be upheld by the ballad writers and singers. The poets obliged and this period in Scottish history duly became enshrined by the idea of the 'Guid Auld Lang Syne,' in other words good times long past.

The ballads produced in the years after 1719 caught the sentimentality of the past, helping to create a unique culture and specific identity.

The poems placed that culture in the never-ending cycle of oppression and resistance that have since become part of our standard view of Scottish history.

These were also the years of the satirical cartoon and the process of lampooning political opponents. That included the members of the royal family. George I, renowned for his mistresses and promiscuous life style, was the subject of many bitter cartoons and effigies that showed him adorned with the horns of a satyr. When his son succeeded him, the lampooning continued.

James, the Old Pretender, and, in due course of time, Charles Edward Stuart were also given 'the treatment' but it lacked the ferocity of the Jacobite satirist cartoonists. It was a lesson well learned – those in power were always more vulnerable to the vitriol of the political critics.

Above all, what the idea of 'Auld Lang Syne' hid from view was the determination of the Scots, their willingness to go to almost any lengths to resist the advances, theoretical and actual, of English power. It was a feeling, an emotion that fuelled the Jacobite cause for many years but one that would also lead to the chaos and disaster of Culloden.

Chapter Eight

The Coming of the Prince and the Lady of Lude

Charles Edward Stuart, the Young Pretender as the Hanoverians sneeringly dubbed him, landed on the island of Eriskay off the west coast of Scotland on 23 July 1745. He was accompanied by just seven supporters, the Seven Men of Moidart as they became known. This was hardly the way Bonnie Prince Charlie had expected or wanted to return to what he still regarded as his homeland, even though he had spent no time at all in the country since his birth in 1720.

In fact, this figurehead of Scottish rebellion and resistance passed only eleven months of his whole life in what he regarded as his 'kingdom'. Most of that time was spent as a fugitive and the rest of it trying not to become one.

He did make a surprising, not to say dangerous, visit to London in 1750 but this was something of an aberration on his part. This surreptitious and secret visit confirmed to him that the Jacobite cause was lost but the trip, which lasted just a few weeks, had little real bearing on his claim to the English throne or on his activities leading up to the launch of the '45 Rebellion.

Charles had returned to France from Italy in 1743 to begin negotiations regarding French help for yet another invasion. Just the year before he had been named as Prince Regent by his father, James III, who was now too old and infirm for prolonged military campaigning. This idea of another landing in Scotland was to be something of a last-ditch attempt to finally put the Old Pretender on the throne of England, Scotland and Ireland.

Charles, like all Jacobites, knew that the longer the Hanoverian dynasty remained in control, the harder they would be to dislodge. Time was running out for the exiled Stuarts and, for that matter, for the representatives of the great European powers who had repeatedly used the Jacobites as pawns in maintaining the balance of power.

Above: Fatherly affection? Or posing for the artist? King Charles I and his younger son James, later James II.

Right: Anne Hyde, first wife of James II. She died without giving James a male heir - much to the delight of English Protestants.

Above: Mary of Modena with her son James - James III as he was officially dubbed, the Old Pretender as he is better known.

Left: Mary of Modena, second wife of James II, and in her own way one of the most important of all Jacobite women.

Above left: King James II in all his glory.

Above right: Lady Nairne, poet and Jacobite to the end of her days.

William of Orange lands, unannounced and unexpected, in the west country, 1688.

The Battle of the Boyne, fought in 1689. William of Orange was wounded in the battle but James fled and never returned to Ireland.

Queen Anne, the last of the Stuart monarchs.

William and Mary, joint monarchs of Britain following the flight of James II and the Glorious Revolution.

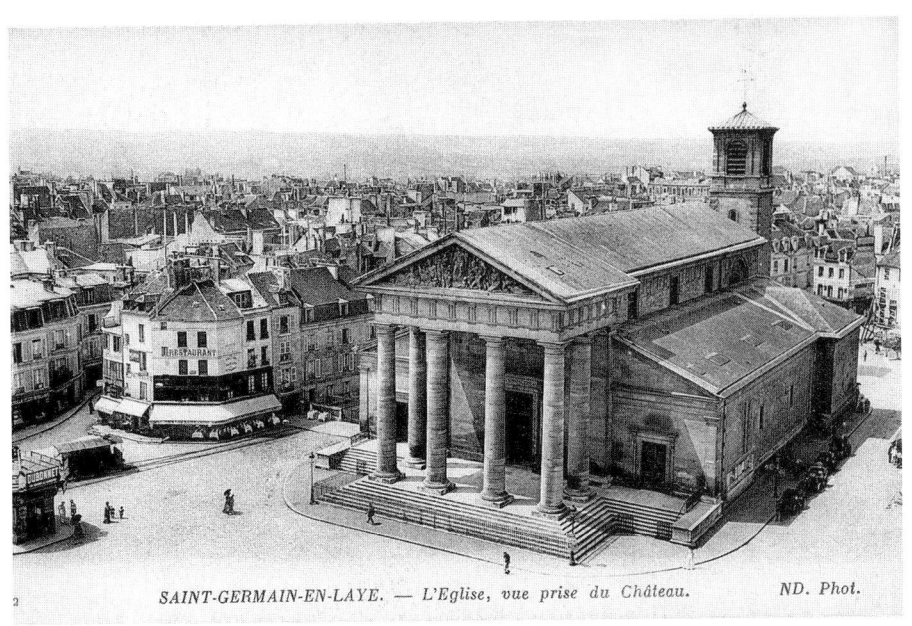

The palatial house outside Paris where James and his family lived following his flight and exile.

JOHN ERSKINE,
EARL OF MARR.
Engraved by M.r Page
FROM A PAINTING BY KNELLER.

Left: The Earl of Mar, leader of the 1715 Rising. Over cautious and unsure he was not the great leader he imagined himself to be.

Below: Castle Eilean Donan, defended by Grizzel Mhor Grant in 1690.

Above left: Jacobite glass, one of many similar souvenirs of the Jacobite risings.

Above right: The much-maligned but brave and headstrong Jenny Cameron.

Rob Roy was one of Scotland's great heroic figures. This shows the remains of his home in the Highlands.

Left: Rob Roy poses for the artist.

Below: The scene of the Glencoe Massacre, a painting by Peter Graham.

The Battle of Glen Shiel.

Above left: Lady Mackintosh, organiser of the Rout of Moy in February 1746. Her five retainers put 1000 redcoats to flight in the action.

Above right: The Tower of London where many Scottish prisoners languished after the various risings. Many of them also escaped from the supposedly stout walls.

A Scottish dwelling house, circa 1745.

Above left: The tomb of Maria Clementia Sabieska, wife of the Old Pretender. A confirmed Catholic, she worked hard to keep the Papacy on the side of the Jacobite's.

Above right: Sir Watkin Williams Wynne, Welsh Jacobite.

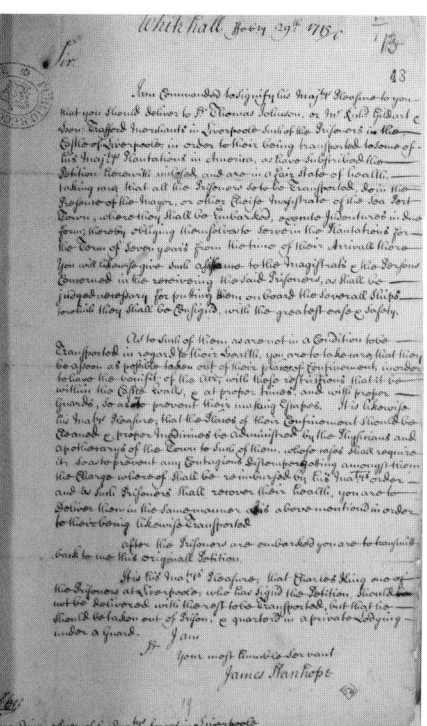

Above left: One of many Jacobite declarations and statements of intent.

Above right: Margaret Ogilvy, escape arranger of the highest order.

James, the Old Pretender, lands at Peterhead for a brief stay of just a few weeks.

The Castle in the Loch. Castles were an important part of the wars and risings but were already beyond their 'sell by' date.

Above left: King George I, the original Hanoverian ruler.

Above right: The Countess of Nithsdale who, finding King George unwilling to help, planned for the escape of her husband from the Tower.

Caroline Oliphant, poet and composer.

Bonnie Prince Charlie addresses his troops.

The landing of Charles Edward Stuart, Bonnie Prince Charlie as he was universally known.

Above: The Battle of Prestonpans, an early success for the Jacobite's but the cause of a bitter dispute between the Prince and his best general.

Left: The classic view of the Young Pretender, handsome, vain but lacking in the skills needed to make a good rival to the Hanoverians.

Below: The final battle, Hanoverian redcoats defeat the Scottish clansmen at the Battle of Culloden.

Above left: Clementina Walkinshaw, mistress to Bonnie Prince Charlie. Abused and ignored, she suffered greatly at the hands of the Prince.

Above right: Butcher Cumberland, hated and feared in equal measures. A portrait by Reynolds.

Right: The one Jacobite woman everyone has heard about, Flora MacDonald.

Flora MacDonald's grave and monument.

The Scottish Clearances, started by Butcher Cumberland, finished by the English parliament, were an attempt to destroy Scottish unity.

Propaganda was used by both sides in what was the great age of satire.

The timing for another invasion was opportune. Robert Walpole, the man who had effectively become Britain's first Prime Minister, had recently been forced out of office by a Whig/Tory alliance – an alliance which the Whigs immediately broke, excluding their political opposites from participation in any form of governance. As a result, there was chaos in British politics with the ousted and bitterly angry Tories appealing to France to come to their aid.

France, as the strongest European nation and as the continental country physically closest to the English coast, had always been the immediate 'go-to' power for the Jacobites when they needed aid and assistance. Only rarely was a request for help turned down and now the appeals of the disenfranchised Tories immediately hit their mark in the French court.

In the autumn of 1743 Louis XV, now King of France, sent James Butler, Master of the King's Horse, to England to spy out the lie of the land and assess the mood of the country. Butler, under the pretext of buying horses for the royal stables, toured southern England and met with many of the leading Tories before returning for a personal interview with Louis.

After much debate and discussion, that November Louis made his decision. A landing would be made in February 1744 by 10,000 French soldiers. They would be ferried in barges hidden along the French coast, to the Maldon area in Essex. From there they would link up with any English Tories who might care to join them to march on London.

Apart from the location of the landing, the plan was, in many respects, a repetition of the old, old story. Amongst other aims there was always the old chestnut of hoping to distract English attention away from their involvement in an ongoing conflict, in this case, the War of the Austrian Succession. The invasion was to be led by the experienced Marshal de Saxe with Charles Edward Stuart, the Young Pretender, as the nominal head of the invasion force. All that the Jacobites had to do was provide pilots with a good knowledge of the tides and sand bars around Maldon.

Charles was happy for the French to launch their assault but there was no way this impetuous young man was ever going to allow them all of the glory. Under his urging the Jacobites would rise and hopefully distract the attention of the British government away from the landings of Marshal de Saxe. It sounded familiar and the French simply shrugged and got on with their own preparations.

The Jacobite Prince was, like his father and grandfather before him, plagued by a shortage of money. He knew what he wanted to do but the money was simply not available. In the end he borrowed 180,000 livres from a Paris bank and even put up the Sobieski Crown, inherited from his mother, as surety for the fitting-out of the two warships that he and his immediate entourage would require for their needs. The two ships were the 66-gun *Elizabeth* and the 16-gun privateer *Du Teillay* which would transport the Prince and his closest followers.

From the beginning, things began to go wrong, as might have been expected given the propensity for bad luck in almost any Stuart enterprise. The British spy network, working feverishly against time, soon uncovered the proposed invasion. It was not entirely unexpected but as Britain and France were not then at war the thought of an invasion before any official declaration had been made angered the Hanoverian government. British warships in the Channel under Admiral Sir John Norris were alerted and put on a state of readiness to attack the approaching French fleet.

The French, for their part, had simply failed to learn from previous mistakes or understand that the Channel in winter was, at best, a fickle mistress. On 24 February, almost as soon as they set sail, the French fleet, carrying almost the entire body of soldiers, ammunition and cannon, ran into a severe gale, arguably the worst storm in living memory. The same storm also hit Norris' ships but they were able to run before the wind and avoid more than one sinking.

In the best traditions of the Spanish Armada and the failed Jacobite invasion of 1708, it was yet another instance of an invader's intentions being foiled by the weather. De Saxe and his commanders fumed but were helpless to do anything other than try to survive.

The fleet was decimated, no fewer than eleven of them going to the bottom, dozens more suffering serious damage. Those that survived, a very bedraggled remainder from what had originally been a powerful force, had no option but to return to France for repairs. It was a disaster:

> Virtually all the supplies and equipment de Saxe had painstakingly accumulated over the previous six months were destroyed. On 28 February Charles Edward was officially informed that the invasion had been cancelled.[1]

Charles now found himself adrift in France. For some months he consoled his battered ego with alcohol and the company of many beautiful women but, gradually, he came to the conclusion that all was not yet lost.

Despite the advice from his closest companions, most of whom made suggestions that he should try again on another day, Charles decided he had gone too far to pull back. He had always fancied the idea of a Jacobite landing without foreign aid and this could be the opportunity he had always dreamed about. He would risk everything, he decided, to try for another incursion.

On 5 July 1745, his two-ship squadron set sail and four days out from France ran into yet more trouble. This time it came, not from the weather but from the bulky shape of a British man-of-war. Spotted by the patrolling *Lion*, the Jacobites found themselves with just two options – they could run or they could stop to fight.

The *Elizabeth* chose the latter but she was outgunned and out-classed by the British vessel. Soon she had received serious damage and had to withdraw from the combat. She managed to limp back to Brest for repairs, taking guns, ammunition and several hundred soldiers of the Irish Brigade with her.

The tiny *Du Teillay* took the other option. The person of Charles Stuart was too important to risk in a sea fight and in a desperate attempt to keep him safe, the captain of the *Du Teillay* decided that discretion was clearly the better part of valour. It was a tactic that was easily put into operation by the French sailors. The *Lion* had been damaged in the encounter with the *Elizabeth*, was herself making water and was in no condition to go chasing the French vessel.

The small but speedy *Du Teillay* soon disappeared over the horizon. Danger still lurked, however, as nobody knew what the privateer might be running into. Had the *Lion* been alone or was she being shadowed by a larger enemy fleet? It was a dangerous few hours for Charles Stuart and his followers.

As it happened, the Jacobites were lucky. There was no British fleet and the western coast of Scotland soon loomed up over the ship's bows. It was an exciting moment for the Prince. However, when he came ashore at Eriskay he was met, not with the enthusiasm he had expected, but with a decidedly cool welcome.

Where were the French, the clan leaders demanded to know? In the early days of planning the invasion Charles had promised to bring at least 3000 French troops with him. Now he was here with just seven comrades. Those clan chiefs who came to meet him were adamant that he should return to France. Defeat, they said, was inevitable and that would cause serious damage to the cause, as well as destruction to their own clans and families. Charles was equally as clear – he was here in Scotland and here he would stay.

After a brief respite, the small Jacobite party boarded the *Du Teillay* once more and, with few regrets, sailed away from Eriskay. They soon anchored in the bay of Loch nan Uamh on the mainland. Unlike his less-than-warm welcome on Eriskay, clansmen now flocked to join him and on 19 August the royal standard of the Stuarts was raised at Glenfinnan. Already there were over 700 Highlanders standing beneath Charles' flag, all ready to swear allegiance to Bonnie Prince Charlie and the Stuart cause.

From Glenfinnan, the Jacobite army marched on Edinburgh. They reached Perth on 4 September and there they paused while more willing sympathisers joined the Prince's band. Command of the army had been given to Lord George Murray and as an experienced general and warrior, he began organising the Jacobite volunteers into something resembling an invasion force.

Sir John Cope, commander of the government troops in Scotland, had 3000 soldiers under his control. Most of them were untrained and un-schooled in the tactics required to fight the Jacobite army but Cope's force was soon enlarged by over 7000 Dutch soldiers who had landed to oppose the Jacobites. However, with the staggering inefficiency of the time – something that affected both Hanoverian and Jacobite leaders – they were never used in combat. In May the following year, the Dutch soldiers returned, unscathed and untroubled, to their base in Holland.

On 17 September the Jacobites entered Edinburgh. Charles paraded in triumph through the streets, grinning, taking salutes and as the centre of everyone's attention-loving every minute of the tumult that greeted him. Despite its decidedly rocky beginning, so far things had gone exactly as Bonnie Prince Charlie had hoped. He held court at Holyrood Palace for the next six weeks and there James III the Old Pretender was announced as King of Scotland, albeit in his absence. Charles was proclaimed Prince Regent.

And yet it was not all plain sailing for the Jacobites. There remained something of a dilemma. They had taken the most significant urban community in Scotland but Edinburgh Castle remained in government hands. The castle on its huge promontory stood barely a mile away from the gathered Jacobites and was a formidable obstacle. Lord George Murray knew that, for the moment anyway, it was best left alone.

The Coming of the Prince and the Lady of Lude

It was a good, old-fashioned stand-off which took little or no notice of the fact that once the main Jacobite force had left Edinburgh the government troops would emerge from the castle and reclaim the town.

* * *

So far Charles and his Jacobite army had made a leisurely progress across the broad belly of Scotland. Although undoubtedly brave, the Young Pretender had already displayed his love of the easy life, 'the wine, women and song' that were later to destroy him. His trip along the Scottish high roads did nothing to repress it. Sleeping under the stars was good for his image, the luxury of a castle or country house was much more appealing. That, the members of his Council decided, could and would be arranged for him.

At the end of August 1745 Charlotte Robertson, the Lady of Lude as she is often known, had received a letter from her cousin William Murray, Marquis of Tullibardine, one of the original Seven Men of Moidart. She should, Tullibardine stated, prepare the castle of Blair Atholl for the arrival of Charles Edward Stuart. Charlotte, a firm and committed Jacobite, was only too pleased to oblige.

Tullibardine had been attainted and disinherited after his involvement in the 1715 Rising, his hereditary estates and castle of Blair Atholl being taken from him and given to his younger brother James. Much to the delight of Charlotte that brother had fled when he heard that the Jacobites were coming. To her, James was a mere stand-in. William Murray would always be the true Duke of Atholl.

Charlotte immediately rode to Blair Atholl, over-riding and brow-beating the servants, greatly annoying them in the process. Charles duly arrived at the castle on the last day of August, halting his army in its march while he was entertained by the Lady of Lude.

Charles stayed in the area for several days, making several visits to Blair Atholl castle to see his admirer. Charlotte later organised an evening entertainment at her own house at Lude for Prince Charles. The Marquis of Tullibardine, Lord George Murray and the rest of the Jacobean hierarchy also attended for the evening. Dinner was followed by a ball where Charlotte, to her utter delight, danced with Charles.

Apparently, Charlotte was in a state of high excitement the whole time the Prince was in the area. And the excitement did not stop with Bonnie

Prince Charlie. At one stage she held a scaling ladder, steadying it and staring upwards while the Highlander soldiers in their kilts climbed up to search for arms in the castle vaults.

According to the vitriolic comments of Thomas Bisset, factor for the new Duke of Atholl, it was impossible to ignore the image of Charlotte gazing up at the men as they climbed. Bissett claimed that he ordered, partly in jest, that only the 'best provided' of the Highlanders should mount the ladder so that she should see only things that were worth seeing. The comment apparently caused the Highlanders to roar with laughter while Charlotte had the good grace to grin and blush – and then stand away from the ladder.

The servants of James, the new Duke of Atholl, had remained behind when he had fled. He could run, they had their positions and jobs to consider. And unlike James, they had nowhere to run to anyway! James' factor, Thomas Bisset, reported regularly to his master, commenting, in particular, on Lady Lude's outlandish behaviour. He clearly did not like the Lady and finding her 'enthusiasm' somewhat disturbing, took every opportunity to embarrass and insult her:

> Lady Lude is here and behaves like a light giglet (a giddy, playful girl), and hath taken upon her to be the sole mistress of the house.[2]

Charlotte was certainly excited and infatuated with the young Prince. When they first met she fell to her knees before him, grabbing his hand and kissing it. Her subsequent behaviour caused considerable comment from the locals, many thinking that she would repeatedly lose her senses whenever she was in the presence of Bonnie Prince Charlie.

Charlotte Robertson, the Lady of Lude, was the first of many women to fawn over Charles Edward Stuart during his sojourn in Scotland. However, his attitude towards his female admirers was strange. He had always enjoyed the attention of women and unashamedly played on their emotions, that was part of his character.

He had mistresses, several of them, but flirting with attractive women was always more interesting for him than any deep and lasting relationship. If he spent anything like an extended period with a woman, he would invariably end up quarrelling with her. And sometimes those quarrels escalated to physical violence. Now, at the beginning of his sojourn in Scotland he was, for some reason, particularly distant and preoccupied – perhaps not surprising considering the seriousness of his task.

Charles Stuart's attitudes and behaviour did not stop women supporters like Charlotte Robertson admiring and flirting with him. Charlotte came from a strong Jacobite family, her mother Lady Nairne being one of the most prominent Jacobite leaders in Perthshire.

Her father had been condemned for treason after the 1715 Rising and incarcerated in the Tower of London to await his fate. The eight-year-old Charlotte visited him in the Tower, a daunting experience for any eight-year-old. Lord Nairne was later reprieved and released but the stain of Jacobitism remained strong in the family, with Charlotte in particular.

Charlotte had married John Robertson of Lude in 1736 but was widowed just six years later. As with many Scottish families at that time money was short and Charlotte had no option but to auction off much of the content of her house.

The sale was overseen by none other than Thomas Bisset who, as well as being factor to the Duke of Atholl, was also Commissary of Dunkeld. The sale went well, many objects being bought by local people. It was a humiliating experience for Charlotte, however, who was even forced to buy back the family beds. Somehow, during the sale she managed to annoy Thomas Bisset, beginning the antagonism that was to last for years.

Charlotte went with the Jacobite army when it finally continued its march. She travelled as far as Dunkeld where she took it upon herself to order the town bells to be rung to welcome Charles Stuart. Returning to Lude, she promptly raised a company of soldiers to join the Atholl Brigade. According to the ever-disagreeable Thomas Bisset, she bullied her tenants to join up, even threatening to hang one reluctant 'volunteer' and promising to burn down the house of another if he did not immediately join her company.[3]

With the war raging across Scotland and northern England, Charlotte Robertson appeared to go quiet for a few months. Then, in February 1746, after the inconclusive Battle of Falkirk, she emerged once again, as if from hibernation.

The Jacobites were now on the back foot and had begun to retreat northwards. Blair Atholl Castle was now occupied by government forces and the Hanoverian army of the Duke of Cumberland plundered the estate at Lude, smashing windows and doors, even ripping up some of the floor boards for firewood. Charlotte Robertson fumed, unable to prevent the destruction but praying that her dancing partner Bonnie Prince Charlie would appear to help. Charles could not oblige, being occupied elsewhere, but his Jacobite comrades eventually did.

In March, Lord George Murray appeared at Lude in command of a detachment of the Atholl Brigade. As part of Jacobite strategy, he had begun attacking several of the government outposts, forts and castles where Hanoverian troops could hold out and challenge Jacobite supply routes. First on the list was Blair Atholl Castle, the assault beginning in the early hours of 17 March.

Charlotte was delighted with the whole operation and when she was given the honour of firing the first cannon shot of the siege her joy knew no bounds. The operation rumbled on with Charlotte, the Lady of Lude, often seen around the Jacobite camp.

According to reports she spent her time giving out brandy to the soldiers, even dancing with them in an attempt to keep their spirits high. However, in the end, it was all for nothing as the walls of the castle were too strong for the lightweight Jacobite artillery. Murray eventually abandoned the siege and slipped quietly away.[4]

In the wake of the failure at Blair Atholl Castle, it was time for retribution. Undoubtedly acting on evidence provided by Thomas Bisset and other servants of the absent Earl of Atholl, Charlotte Robertson was arrested. She was brought before Sir Andrew Agnew, newly appointed commander of the Blair Atholl garrison, and was duly interrogated.

However, things did not go exactly how Bisset and other informers had planned. Charlotte managed to charm Andrew Agnew and after giving her dinner, he sent her back home. He even apologised to her for the inconvenience he had caused. And there, for the moment, things rested.

After Culloden and the end of the Jacobite rising it was rumoured that Charlotte and her mother, Lady Nairne, were going to be arrested and put on trial for taking part in the rebellion. It did not happen and Charlotte died in 1787, just a year before her hero Bonnie Prince Charlie.

Caroline Robertson, the Lady of Lude, never lost her Jacobite sympathies even when all prospect of a Stuart restoration had long since gone. Her clashes with Thomas Bisset undoubtedly helped to blacken her reputation but there is no denying her position as one of the first Jacobite supporters to 'come out' in favour of Charles Edward Stuart.

Chapter Nine

Culloden and the Women of the Battlefield

The first real contact between Bonnie Prince Charlie's Jacobites and the Hanoverian forces of the British government occurred on 21 September at the Battle of Prestonpans.

Also known as the Battle of Gladsmuir after the muddy marshland over which it was fought, the encounter lasted less than half an hour. It saw the Hanoverian troops broken, fleeing for their lives, and leaving the Jacobites in command of the field. Inevitably, the build-up to the battle was somewhat more protracted.

In August 1745, hearing of the gathering of the clans at Glenfinnan, General Sir John Cope left his artillery and cavalry at Stirling and moved his infantry swiftly across country, aiming to occupy the Corrieyairack Pass between the Highlands and Lowlands ahead of the Jacobites. When he arrived at Corrieyairack, he found the Jacobites already in occupation and so withdrew to Inverness where he was reunited with his artillery and cavalry forces.

A few days later Cope learned that the Jacobites were marching on Edinburgh. Deciding to intercept them, he loaded his troops onto ships and sailed out of Aberdeen aiming to come ashore at Dunbar. He landed his force on 17 September, exactly the same day as Bonnie Prince Charlie entered Edinburgh. Despite the loss of Scotland's capital, Cope was confident that his 3000 professional soldiers could outmatch the 2000 Highlanders under Lord George Murray. It was a clear case of over-confidence and, as it turned out, Cope was gravely mistaken.

The two armies drew up facing each other just outside Prestonpans to the east of Edinburgh, separated by a large tract of marshy ground. Murray knew that if he allowed his men to charge – as they so desperately wanted – they would become bogged down in the mud and consequently expose themselves to enemy musket and cannon fire. Instead, he took his men on a circuitous route, shown to him by one of the local population, and caught Cope's troops on their flank. The sudden attack took the Hanoverian troops totally by surprise.

It was the perfect time for the famous Highland charge and, at last, Murray unleashed his shock force. The charge of the Highlanders was unstoppable and resulted in over 400 dead Hanoverians. The Jacobites, in contrast, lost less than forty killed and wounded. Cope's poorly trained levies had proved no match for the fearsome Jacobite assault. It was a remarkable victory, one that provided a huge morale boost for the Jacobites, but it was marred by a serious argument between Charles Edward Stuart and Lord George Murray.

Prince Charles Edward Stuart had wanted to charge immediately, as soon as he saw Cope's force, ignoring the marsh which lay between the two armies. It was an impetuous idea, typical of the Prince, and would have meant utter disaster. The more experienced Murray knew that his flank attack was the only way and over-ruled the Prince. It was a successful tactic but the argument soon began to destroy the already brittle and acrimonious relationship that existed between the two men. And that would go on to have serious consequences later in the campaign.

The government reacted swiftly to news of the defeat. William, Duke of Cumberland, youngest son of George II, was recalled from Flanders where he had been leading the British forces in various campaigns as part of the War of the Austrian Succession. He was experienced, decisive and, as it soon turned out, brutal in his approach to war. He brought with him 12,000 trained and experienced soldiers, men who were used to his harsh discipline and to the effects of intense fighting. The war against the Jacobites had clearly moved up a notch or two.

In the wake of the Prestonpans victory, in October 1745 Bonnie Prince Charlie issued two Declarations, the first dissolving the hated union of 1707 and the second denying the Act of Settlement. The Prince's Council, an advisory body of approximately twenty leading Jacobites, now began to debate the next move for the army.

Most of the Scots on the Council wanted to consolidate their position and revive the pre-1707 Scottish Parliament. For Prince Charles, however, an invasion of England was essential, not only as a decisive step towards establishing his father on the throne but, short term, of gaining more French help towards the creation of an independent Scotland. The Irishmen in his command agreed with Charles. After all, putting the Stuarts back on the throne was one significant step in re-establishing the

Catholic religion in their country and as James, the Old Pretender had promised, creating a totally independent Ireland.

The debate raged for some time. Eventually a decision was made. England would be invaded but only if the French and the English Jacobites gave practical assistance, the French with an invasion, English Jacobites with a rising. Charles assured everyone that such support would indeed be forthcoming, he was already in touch with his English counterparts and they were merely awaiting his arrival. It was, of course, an outright lie.

By now Charles Edward Stuart had already alienated a large number of his immediate supporters and comrades. He was, those supporters were discovering, arrogant and opinionated, haughty, and unwilling to take advice. He needed to be kept in check but almost all of the Council Members were at a loss about how to do it.

The Prince was also, the majority of the Scots felt, too close to the Irish, too willing to take their side in any argument. As a result, factions were beginning to develop in the Jacobite ranks and neither Charles Stuart himself nor the Jacobite general George Murray possessed the correct degree of humility or the social skills to redress the situation.

Reinforced by a small number of French troops who landed in Scotland in October, the Jacobites left Edinburgh on 4 November. As predicted, government forces in the castle immediately emerged to retake the city the moment the Jacobites left.

Lord George Murray decided not to take the traditional route south via Berwick on Tweed but, in order to deceive General Wade who was then commanding the garrison in Newcastle, he would move down the western side of the country. That would take the army through territory that was supposedly violently pro-Jacobite. The army marched in two columns, numbering around 4000, and entered England unopposed four days later.

It was a clever ploy by Murray but one that was, strangely, resented by the Prince who seemed to vacillate between sulking and outright anger in his dealings with his most efficient military commander:

> Charles was aware of his debt to Murray and bitterly resented it. He could not brook sustained opposition to his will, still less reasoned, cogent criticism of his plans, and

thus by the time the crucial council of war came, at Derby on 5 December, it was well known that Charles and his best general were barely on speaking terms.[1]

The border town of Carlisle, garrisoned by a small force of just 80 veterans and old men, was open to the Jacobites and duly surrendered on 15 November. Murray left a small detachment to hold the castle and town and marched on.

On 26 November the army reached Preston, entering Manchester two days later. Despite his reluctance to head south into England, Murray had done a superb job and yet there was a sense of foreboding and unease in the Jacobite ranks.

The march south had not garnered them anything like the number of recruits they had expected. Apart from Manchester which offered up enough volunteers to form the Manchester Regiment, there was a marked lack of enthusiasm from almost all the other towns they passed. Preston, supposedly a Jacobite hotbed, had provided just three recruits.[2]

It was hugely disappointing and many of the Scottish leaders were adamant that they wanted to go back. They could defend Scotland, they reasoned, but this march into England was across unknown territory. They were putting themselves out on a limb.

The Prince managed to persuade them to continue the march, promising that the Welsh Jacobite leader Sir Watkin Williams-Wynn would join them, with reinforcements, at Derby. The French were almost ready to launch yet another invasion, Charles declared. Not only that, the Duke of Beaufort was preparing to besiege the port and city of Bristol.

The Scots reluctantly agreed to continue with the march and by 4 December the rebel army had reached the midlands town of Derby. There was no sign of the Welsh Jacobites and no indication that Sir Watkin had ever intended to join them there. Equally as disturbing, there was no news from the Duke of Beaufort or from Bristol. Perhaps inevitably, of the French there was no sign. An emergency meeting of the Prince's Council was called for 5 December.

The meeting was more than a little uncomfortable for the Prince. He had no option but to admit lying about English risings and about French landings in support of the Jacobite army. Without these Murray, declared, they could not proceed southwards. Already the Duke of

Cumberland stood between them and London and with General Wade rapidly coming up in the Jacobite rear there was a very real danger of being outflanked and surrounded.

There had actually been a French landing in Montrose. Originally thought to consist of over 3000 troops it really numbered just 700 men and was basically inconsequential as far as the march south was concerned. Bonnie Prince Charlie was furious at the attitudes of the Scottish leaders. They had achieved so much, he argued and were now sat in the centre of England, ready to attack London. It was an impassioned and logical argument but the Scottish Jacobites were in no mood to listen:

> The Prince heard all these arguments with the greatest impatience, fell into a passion and gave most of the gentlemen that had spoken very abusive language.[3]

He then went into a sulk of monumental proportions and declared that he would never call the Council again. In this he was true to his word, the Council never met again. As far as this meeting was concerned, a vote was taken and, with the Prince being the only one to cast his lot for continuing with the march south it was decided that the Jacobite army would turn around and head north, back to Scotland.

* * *

It was a bitter blow for Prince Charles and for many of the diehard Jacobites in the ranks of the army. Charles refused to have anything more to do with the campaign, retreated to his tent and resorted to the whiskey and brandy bottles to keep himself occupied. Meanwhile, General George Murray performed brilliantly and by employing a range of different manoeuvres managed to keep the Jacobite army out of Cumberland's clutches.

There was one brief skirmish at Clifton Moor early in 1746 and then Murray began to besiege Stirling Castle. He had been equipped with newly acquired French cannons, the previous lack of such weapons having proved one of the significant factors in helping the Jacobite leaders make the decision to retreat.

The siege eventually lasted for two months before the advance of government forces along the road from Edinburgh caused the Jacobites to end the attack. Even a victory over a Hanoverian relief force under Henry Hawley at the Battle of Falkirk Muir could not help the situation and with many of the Highlanders now abandoning the army and heading for home it was clear that the invasion was as good as over.

The Duke of Cumberland re-took Carlisle early in 1746, the last Jacobite stronghold or presence in England. He entered Edinburgh on 30 January while those Jacobites who remained with the rebel army were intent on retreating to Inverness. After a brief respite in Edinburgh, the Duke of Cumberland moved slowly northwards along the coast, arriving in Aberdeen at the end of February. There he paused to fine-tune his tactics and re-equip his forces.

From this point on defeat for the Jacobites was inevitable. It was merely a matter of time, with Murray pre-occupied with trying to save as many of his soldiers as possible and Bonnie Prince Charlie still sulking in his tent.

Brilliantly as Murray had performed during the retreat, in February he missed a golden opportunity to attack government forces without their leader being present. Cumberland had been briefly recalled to London when rumours of a French invasion began to assume concrete proportions. With the threat of a French landing suddenly becoming very real indeed, he was needed to defend Westminster and Parliament.

The French threat was no piece of wishful thinking. The Duc de Richelieu had gathered over 10,000 troops under his command at Boulogne where he was assisted by Charles' brother Henry Benedict Stuart. Regardless of the quantity and quality of the French troops, involving Henry was undoubtedly a mistake as Charles' younger brother was more interested in theology and his own personal religious stance than in preparations for war. In fact, Richelieu found Henry's pious nature and beliefs to be quite offensive. Bad feelings, it seemed, were not confined to George Murray and Bonnie Prince Charlie.

By the beginning of February, the officers of the proposed invasion force had taken to bickering amongst themselves and when bad weather struck the Channel ports all thoughts of invasion were abandoned. Despite letters from King Louis ordering the invasion to begin, Richelieu's army was duly disbanded.[4]

Cumberland immediately returned to Scotland where he gathered his troops at Nairne, ready for the final showdown against Prince Charles and his depleted army. In April 1746 Bonnie Prince Charlie, emerging at last from his tent and perhaps realising that the end was close, insisted on one last throw of the dice. He and his Jacobite army would face the Duke of Cumberland on Drummossie Moor at Culloden outside Inverness.

The Battle of Culloden took place on 16 April 1746. It was the last pitched battle ever to be fought on the British mainland and, from the beginning, it proved to be a disaster for the Jacobite forces.

The night before the engagement the Duke of Cumberland gave out two barrels of brandy to each of his regiments so that they could celebrate his birthday in style. The government forces were therefore happy, relaxed and content. That was clearly not the case in the Jacobite ranks.

Bonnie Prince Charlie had suggested a night attack, a tactic that had worked for the Jacobites before. As Cumberland's force now outnumbered the Jacobite army by almost two to one Lord George Murray reluctantly agreed. It was, he felt, going to be their last chance of victory.

Relations between Murray and the Prince were still not good and that morning they reached their zenith. Murray had been stripped of his position in charge of battlefield operations, those duties having been purloined by the Prince and his new favourite, the Irish quartermaster John William O'Sullivan.

While Cumberland's men were lying happily in their tents and bivouacs, swigging down their copious supplies of brandy, the half-starved Jacobites were marching through the night, attempting to get into position for the attack on government forces in Nairne. From the beginning, it had proved to be an impossible task.

Delays, poor leadership, and lack of direction caused chaos in the Jacobite ranks. Units became separated, men found themselves lost and out of touch with their comrades, so that when they did finally draw up for battle at Culloden early on 16 April they were exhausted and half frozen by the snow and hail that had fallen on them during their mindless 'night rambles' Not only that, the Prince had chosen an entirely inappropriate site for the battle:

> The Prince, using his crony John William O'Sullivan as military advisor, had decided to offer battle on Culloden Moor. As Lord George Murray pointed out, no more

disastrous choice for Highlanders could be imagined, as it was open moorland, affording full scope for the enemy's superiority in cannon, and none at all for the clansmen's devastating charge.[5]

With the first light of dawn beginning to gleam in the eastern sky, Lord George Murray had already suggested abandoning the night attack. There was, he explained to the Prince, clearly not enough time to get into position. His advice was ignored. It showed the state of relationships at the head of the Jacobite army, the active dislike between Murray and the Prince being a major factor in the defeat awaiting them on Culloden Moor.

By the morning of the battle, Bonnie Prince Charlie seemed to have recovered some of his determination and desire for victory over the Hanoverians. It might have been misdirected but, for the moment, his sulking forgotten and regardless of Murray's pleas and advice, the Prince was clear. He was going to fight and this time he was going to win.

Despite the confidence of the Prince, by the morning of 16 April when the troops began drawing up for battle, it can be argued that the Jacobites were already beaten. Due to the chaotic night manoeuvres to which they had been subjected, nearly one third of the rebel army was adrift in the countryside, sleeping in ditches, totally exhausted and demoralised. It meant that a large part of the Jacobite force would take no part in the coming battle. It was a weakness, a lack of soldiers, that the rebels could not afford and what followed was a complete and utter fiasco for the Jacobites.

The Duke of Cumberland had struck camp at 5.00 am and begun a forced march across country to Culloden. Those Jacobites who had made it to the battlefield watched as the enemy marched across the moor and drew up in front of them. As was traditional they hurled insults and cries at the government troops but this time they were answered only by a stony silence which was chilling in its intensity.

The battle began at 1.00 pm when Jacobite artillery opened fire, quickly returned by the heavier and more effective government cannons. Cumberland's men were using canister shot that exploded in the air above the Highlander's ranks, the shrapnel causing havoc in the waiting lines. There was no respite from the hail of missiles and soon the Jacobite army began to lose shape as man after man was mown down.

In the wake of his artillery bombardment, Cumberland decided to unleash his dragoons. It was a largely ineffective move as the heavy marshland of the battlefield impeded the movement of their horses. In good order, the dragoons fell back but then came the decisive moment of the whole action. The Highlanders charged.

Screaming their battle cry of 'Claymore', the clansmen raced towards the government lines. The charge of the Highlanders had, over the past decade or so, become an unbeatable tactic, one which broke the spirit and the arms of opponents. Not this time.

The Highlanders got to within 100 yards before the cannon and musket fire of the enemy cut them to ribbons. The left section of their line crumpled as the Jacobite elite turned, and ran back in headlong retreat; the right-hand columns raced on but failed to break the government line and were forced back from the contact point, albeit in a more orderly retreat. The much-feared charge of the Highlanders had failed in the face of superior fire power and greater discipline.

Both sections of the Jacobite line were harried by Cumberland's cavalry and dragoons as they fell back and it took two strong rear-guard actions by the Irish on the left, the Lifeguards on the right, to allow at least some of the Highlanders to escape the carnage.

Bonnie Prince Charlie was led from the field, proclaiming that the Hanoverians would never take him alive. His battered army retreated to the north and, in some cases, to the south. The battle was over. It had lasted barely half an hour.[6]

* * *

The battle might have been over but the killing was certainly not. In the wake of the Jacobite demise the Duke of Cumberland immediately set about earning his nickname, Bloody Cumberland. He was named after ordering his infamous 'no prisoners' policy in the wake of the Jacobite defeat. It was an attempt on the part of the Duke to wipe out all traces of Jacobitism which, by its very existence, was a significant threat to the Hanoverian dynasty.

Cumberland did attempt to justify his actions. He declared that he had ordered 'No prisoners' only when it became known that Charles

Edward Stuart had given the similar command of 'No quarter' to his troops. In fact, no such order ever came from the Jacobite ranks.

As a consequence of Cumberland's order, wounded Highlanders were bayoneted, knifed or shot where they lay, their bodies then left to rot on the field of battle. So Bloody Cumberland it was. The Whigs, supporters of the Hanoverian government, retaliated by dubbing him Sweet William. That epithet seems now to have disappeared; Bloody Cumberland remains in common use!

Casualties amongst the Jacobites were high. Estimates vary between 1700 and 2000 dead, many of these coming in the after-battle furore which turned a military engagement into a massacre. In complete contrast, the government casualty figure was just 300.

The female camp followers were quickly on the scene of the massacre, tending to the wounded and spiriting away as many Highlanders as possible before the government forces despatched them. Even now, most of these women remain guarded by the usual shield of anonymity and so we do not know the names of far too many of them.

Prison records in jails like Carlisle, Chester, Lancaster, and York show that after Culloden at least 56 women and girls were confined within their walls for various lengths of time, accused of supporting the last Jacobite rebellion. These would have been the camp followers, women who were brave enough to defy the threat of Hanoverian bayonets but without the means to run, hide or gain support from influential citizens. It would have been temporary confinement for these women, most of them being transported to America and the West Indies in the months and years after the Jacobite defeat.

However, the names of one or two of these victims of 'Hanoverian justice' are recorded. Included amongst them were Agnes Cathel who was transported along with her three-year-old child and Agnes Flint who had been attached to Major Glenbucket's Regiment. She was accompanied into exile by her seven-year-old child. Mary Kennedy was kept in prison for several months before being sent to the West Indies along with her ten-year-old son.[7]

In all, twenty-eight women were sent to the American colonies and to West Indian islands such as Antigua following the failure of the rebellion. None of them were granted the curtesy of a trial, most of them being transported on the slave ship *Veteran*. She sailed in the year 1747, meaning that by the time they were deported the women had already languished in one prison or another for two long years.

By sheer unlucky chance, the transport ship *Veteran* was intercepted and captured by a French privateer. That should have meant freedom for the women and new homes in France but the fate and eventual destination of the Jacobite women remains unknown. Some probably did make it to France, others to the West Indies but the fate of the majority remains unclear.

It was not just the camp followers who tried to help the wounded and dying Highlanders at Culloden. Anne Leith was a young widow from the area around Aberdeen who, in the spring of 1746, was lodging at Inverness. When she heard news of the battle about to take place on Culloden Moor, she immediately knew that she had to help. She collected together bandages, splints, soothing creams and balms, and in the company of a friend called Mrs Stoner and a maid by the name of Eppy, set off for the battlefield.[8]

The three women walked straight into what can only be regarded as a scene from Hell. Wounded and dying Highlanders were strewn across the field while Hanoverian redcoats strutted about bayoneting any of them that moved. Without qualms the women immediately set to work, binding wounds, and giving what solace they could to fatally wounded men.

It was an unpleasant task that would have terrified many people but not Anne Leith and Mrs Stoner. Their task was not just daunting, it was also dangerous as, hours after the conflict ended, the Hanoverian soldiers were still roaming the battlefield, looking for Jacobites to finish off. And to them it did not matter if the prospective victim was a soldier or a civilian, a man or a woman.

The work of Anne Leith did not end on 17 April. She continued to offer help for three or four months after the battle, constantly visiting the prisons and jails where those Jacobites who had managed to survive the murder on the moor were being held. She distributed food, bandaged sores and wounds, all the time protesting about the inhuman treatment of the prisoners.

Anne's activities cost her what little money she had – and it also cost her several friendships with relatives and with people who were neither so generous with their time and resources nor so taken with the Jacobite cause.[9]

If Anne Leith lost friends through her activities, she also gained many new ones from amongst the ranks of Jacobite supporters and former participants in the battle. Many of them wrote to her in the years after Culloden. She was given a nickname, the Grand Rebel.

She continued to annoy and antagonise the government troops and officials. She was arrested on a number of occasions, albeit for fairly minor infringements. Anne seemed to have something of a golden tongue in her mouth and always managed to talk her way out of trouble, rarely being held for more than a day or so.

Ignoring the attentions of officers and other officials who regularly intercepted and read her mail, Anne Leith also made friends with several of the government officials who, despite being the enemy, regarded her as a more than worthy opponent. They admired her stance and her actions, and saw her as a woman of great courage and compassion.

Anne Leith was not alone. Anne McKay hailed from the Isle of Skye but was living in the cellar of the Inverness Tollbooth at the time of the battle and its aftermath. She not only provided one badly wounded Jacobite soldier, Robert Nairn, with clothes and sanctuary, she flirted with his guard and got him very drunk. She then walked the unsuspecting jailer into nearby woodland and 'occupied him' while Nairn made good his escape.

Another Jacobite she tried to help, Captain Ronald Macdonald, had sustained such terrible injuries to his legs that he could not walk. Unable to manage the escape, Macdonald had to be left behind. He later died in captivity.

Anne was arrested and charged with helping Nairne to escape. She was offered a bribe of ten guineas to confess and name other local women who were also helping the Jacobites. Anne refused and consequently was thrown into the Bridge Hole, a coffin-shaped cellar room in the Tollbooth prison with traffic thundering by overhead.

Made to stand upright for three days, Anne McKay suffered greatly. Her legs swelled so much that she could barely walk. Still she would not talk.

Next came threats, which also proved unsuccessful. Finally, the sentries contrived a plot – they would get her drunk so that her tongue would be loosened! An Irish soldier's wife sent her whiskey but Anne was too wise to fall for the trick. 'I only drink milk and whey,' she declared and refused the gift.

Apart from the offer of whiskey, Anne was also deprived of all food and drink, and made the subject of vicious and prolonged verbal assaults from the soldiers and jailers. Finally, seven weeks after her imprisonment began, the guards gave up. Anne was released from the Bridge Hole and allowed to spend the rest of her captivity in the Tollbooth.

Robert Nairne's unlucky guard may have enjoyed his brief flirtation with Anne but in the wake of his few minutes of fun reality hit home. He was given five hundred lashes and Anne, who was also sentenced to a public lashing, was kept in detention at the Tollbooth for seven weeks.

In the end, Anne's flogging was not carried out – partly due to the appeals and efforts of Lady Mackintosh – but even after her release, she continued to suffer. Her son, just seventeen years old, was attacked and beaten so severely by government soldiers that he died two or three days after the assault.[10]

On her release Anne McKay moved to Inverness and in 1748 contributed an account of her treatment to Robert Forbes's book on the rebellion. Entitled *Lyon in Mourning*, the book was unashamedly pro-Jacobite in its stance and outlook.

Anne continued to support the exiled Stuarts, even refusing to drink the health of the Duke of Cumberland when ordered to do so by the government officials.

Hiding escapees and fugitives from government searches was a common enough occurrence in the post-Culloden period. Women of the Haldane family near Doune turned it into what was a virtual art form, albeit with a little assistance from sympathetic government officials:

> One of the young daughters of the house, not understanding the danger, proudly showed one man what she'd discovered – the cheeses out of sight under the bed for conveying to the Jacobite fugitives - - -When the child's aunt came back into the room, the soldier told her quietly "Do not let that child be left alone again. Had she shown another what she has shown to me, it would have brought you into trouble."[11]

What began with kindness and compassion sometimes finished with love. Elizabeth Eyre helped prisoners in Southwark, London, and in the course of her regular visits fell in love with the Jacobite Francis Farquharson. Sentenced to death, Farquharson was given a reprieve on the condition he did not go back to Scotland. He married Elizabeth and the pair lived contentedly in Berkhamsted for many years.

In the summer of 1746 Elizabeth Grant and Edmund Clavering were married by a Catholic Priest who, like them, was imprisoned in York Castle. The wedding infuriated the authorities who were unable to do anything about it – both parties were of an appropriate age and the Priest was acting in his official capacity.

As it turned out, the marriage was a short-term affair. Edmund, 'half mad-man, as well as whole rebel', as he was described, went to the gallows in November 1746. Elizabeth was held in York until the summer of 1747. No mean rebel herself, she was then transported to the West Indies.

For those women who remained incarcerated in prisons, even in The Tower of London, life was far from pleasant. Amazingly, several women went solemnly but deliberately into confinement along with their husbands. It was cheaper than lodging outside and with the prospect of execution hanging over their partners, it was a last chance of at least a little affection.

Lady Cromarty, widely known as Bonnie Belle, travelled south with her three daughters in order to support her husband George who was lingering in the Tower under a sentence of death.

To begin with, she was not allowed into the prison and had to console herself with the seemingly pointless task of writing letters to her husband.

After petitioning the Duke of Newcastle, Bonnie Belle and her daughters were given permission to sit with Lord Cromarty and her brother John who was also in the Tower, for up to ten hours every day. Bonnie Belle and her daughters were finally allowed to move in and live with George in a warder's house inside the Tower.

Lord Cromarty was later reprieved and released from his imprisonment but the Tower had not finished with his wife. At one stage she was examined by the official Tower Doctors due to fears that she might be pregnant. She was not alone. The wife of Captain Patrick Wallace actually gave birth to a daughter while they were living together in the Tower. It was, you might say, an occupational or imprisonment hazard.

There were many instances of Jacobite women helping prisoners and escapees, some humorous, some tragic. In many respects they are the stuff of comic books. One of the more amusing tales concerned Mrs Lumsden, wife of a Presbyterian minister.

She and her husband were hiding escaped prisoners and moving them on to other safe houses when the coast was clear. However, maids in the parsonage complained that food was going short and that they had seen shadows flitting across the walls in the night. Soon the mysterious happenings were common knowledge. Mrs Lumsden explained it away very easily.

The shortage of food in the kitchen, she said, well that was simple. It was down to nothing more than the extra rations she had been giving to two pigs she had been fattening up ready for market. And the shadows? They were just ghosts. The maids were immediately terrified into silence and all investigation into the complaints was dropped.[12]

Chapter Ten

Jacobite Women, Heroes of the '45

It is probably an inevitable fact of social life in the eighteenth century that we know a lot more about the middle- and upper-class ladies who helped Bonnie Prince Charlie than we are ever likely to do about the ordinary working-class women of the time. In the main, their stories are the stuff of legend, fascinating, compelling but still humane – and not always the exact honest truth.

Some are stories of deep involvement; some are stories with tentative connections to the Jacobite rising. Regardless of their content, they were all important, all part of the Jacobite experience, at one level or another. There are many such tales, many such women, but try these for size.

Jean/Jenny Cameron

It is difficult to know where and when the story of Jean or Jenny Cameron moves from fact to fiction. There have been so many tales about her life, many, if not most of them, invented by the Hanoverian supporters, and yet – and yet?

She was a significant figure in the '45 Rising and the Hanoverians chose to spread stories about her lewd behaviour and ravenous sexual appetite as a way of demeaning both her and the Jacobite cause. There is probably a degree of truth in some of the stories but no real way of telling.

What is known is that she was the eldest daughter of Hugh Cameron of Glendesseray and was something of a wild child. At the age of eleven, she was sent to live in Edinburgh with an aunt who was charged with trying to teach her how to behave like a lady. After a promising start this eventually became a pointless exercise as, within a year or so, the aunt's footman and her household maid began to show Jenny the more disreputable side of the city.

When she was caught carousing in one of these less acceptable areas, the young Jenny Cameron was thrown into jail where she kicked her heels until bailed out by her aunt. Confined to the house, Jenny behaved herself until she was eventually found in bed with the footman. He, incidentally, was sacked! Still only sixteen, Jenny apparently found herself pregnant, had a miscarriage and, in desperation, was packed off to a nunnery in France. Fact or fiction, we simply do not know the true extent of that piece of her history.

After numerous amorous adventures, including time spent in Flanders with an Irish soldier who abandoned her and left her alone and destitute, Jenny Cameron wound up back in Scotland. There she lived with her brother and his wife – until, the Hanoverians gleefully claimed, she was found in bed with the brother. Once again, the story probably owes more to the art of black propaganda than it does to actual fact.

The invasion of '45 saw Jenny at Glenfinnan when the clans mustered. It also saw her pledge her support for Bonnie Prince Charlie by bringing him 200 men and a herd of cows from the family estate. By now she was in her mid-forties but was still regarded as a very handsome woman. She was described as 'decked with green furniture tinted with gold, her hair tied back in a loose buckle, with a velvet cap and a scarlet feather.'[1]

Jenny became a favourite at Prince Charles' court and accompanied the army on its journey to battle at Prestonpans. Clad in men's tartan trews and carrying an unsheathed sword, one version of her activities has Jenny leading the attack at the forefront of the Jacobite line. Given her enjoyment of adventure, it is more than likely that she was at the Battle of Prestonpans but the idea of her leading the rush of the Highlanders in their charge is probably, once again, more fiction than fact.

Jenny Cameron was captured when Stirling Castle was taken in February 1746. Imprisoned for a short while she was later released but was never fully trusted by the Hanoverian government, members of which viewed her as a threat to stability in Scotland. The government thought that by deriding her conduct and blackening her name they would be reducing Jenny Cameron to a laughing stock. In fact, the direct opposite occurred, Jenny quickly assuming the role of femme fatale. It did not stop the Hanoverians spreading their tales.

Indeed, more stories about her reckless and feckless life style were put about and as late as 1753 government agents were still keeping a close watch on her. She died, renowned by many, feared by some, lusted after by almost everyone, in 1773.

Lady Mackintosh (AKA Colonel Anne)

Anne Farquharson came from the strongly Jacobite Clan Farquharson and so it is a little surprising that she should marry Angus Mackintosh, chief of the politically opposite Mackintoshes. Compared to some of the Scottish clans both the Farquharsons and the Mackintoshes were relatively small family groupings. They were, however, part of the larger Chattan Confederation, a community of twelve small clans who pledged their allegiance to their own clan chief and to the head of the Chattans.

The Mackintoshes were, in general, pro-Hanoverian government supporters and therefore stood on the opposite side of the battle lines from the Farquharsons when, in 1745, Bonnie Prince Charlie arrived in Scotland. Angus Mackintosh immediately enlisted in the Black Watch, Highlander militia men who were fighting for the government. Anne regretfully watched him ride off but remained determined to stay loyal to her own beliefs.

When Prince Charles passed close by on his march towards Edinburgh, Anne hosted him at Moy Hall, the family home of her and her husband. She then spent several weeks riding around the area, raising troops for the Young Pretender and his army.

Prince Charles visited Moy Hall once again in February 1746, this time during his retreat to Inverness. Again, he was made welcome and treated to a lavish banquet prepared by Anne's staff. The Prince, still sulking after the decision to withdraw from England, managed to emerge from his 'cocoon' in order to enjoy the event before falling into his first soft bed in weeks.

At 5.00 am on 17 February a messenger came hammering at the door of Moy Hall. He was the fifteen-year-old Lachlan Mackintosh, sent by an unknown person in the Inverness garrison with a warning for Lady Anne and for Bonnie Prince Charlie. Government forces under Lord Loudon, the young Lachlan managed to gasp out, were advancing on the house, having been told that the Prince was resting there. Loudon was intending to capture the Prince and, at the same time, claim the £30,000 reward on his head.

Anne Mackintosh had no soldiers at her disposal but she did have copious amounts of native wit. Dressed only in her shift, she ran through the house, calling her staff together. She then ordered five of them, led by the Moy blacksmith Donald Fraser, into the woods that flanked the approach road. Their task was simple – to make enough noise to convince the approaching Hanoverian troops that they were walking into an ambush.

The night was dark, the sky illuminated by occasional flashes of lightning. Peat stacks and trees cast long shadows each time the lightning flashed, totally unnerving the approaching government troops. And then the noise began, orders and shouts that echoed around the road and woods.

The men of Lady Anne's 'army' were in position when Loudon and his 1500 soldiers, led by piper Donald Ban McCrimmon, came tiptoeing into view. Donald Fraser opened fire and the piper toppled over dead. The rest of the government soldiers, convinced that they were facing a large Jacobite force, immediately fell back.

When Fraser shouted for his men to advance, Loudon and his troops took to their heels and ran for their lives. The staggering success of five men against 1500, along with the genius of Lady Anne, went down in history as The Rout of Moy.

Two days later Bonnie Prince Charlie took control of Inverness. Amongst his prisoners was Angus Mackintosh. The Prince remanded him into the company of his wife with the comment 'You could not be in better security.'

Anne's acceptance of the task was immediate, her reply was simple – 'Your servant, Captain,' she told her husband. He replied with the words 'Your servant, Colonel'. The name stuck and thereafter Anne Mackintosh was known by the epithet of Colonel Anne.[2]

Like Jenny Cameron before her, Anne Mackintosh suffered the ignominy of Hanoverian propaganda, being labelled as promiscuous and lewd in her behaviour.

Aged only twenty-two at the time of the Rout of Hoy, she was a beautiful woman and Lord Loudon certainly had something of a crush on her. Anne was more than capable of using his infatuation but there is no evidence of extra-marital affairs either with him or anyone else.

Lady Drummuir

The identity of the sender of the warning message to Lady Anne Mackintosh and Prince Charles at Moy Hall, and therefore precipitator of the Rout of Hoy, remains unknown.

However, the most popular contender for the title is Katherine Duff, the Lady Drummuir of Inverness. As in so much of Jacobite history, there is no definite proof but an in-built desire to help would certainly have been an essential part of her character.

A strong-minded woman, Lady Drummuir was also caring and compassionate. Every Sunday on her way to church she would apparently distribute copper coins to the value of two or three shillings to the poor of the town. Her generosity became so well known that those in need would sit on stools outside the church, waiting for their benefactor to appear.

Her connection to the Jacobite cause seems limited to the possible warning but, if nothing else, she warrants a mention because of a well-known throwaway line attributed to her.

Lady Drummuir owned one of the finest town houses in Inverness, a solid and gracious-looking building in Crown Street, so well situated and comfortable that both Bonnie Prince Charlie and the Duke of Cumberland took the house as their headquarters during the Culloden campaign. Indeed, it was said that they had both used the same bed!

The house had been commandeered and Lady Drummuir's comment on her unasked-for guests was simple but telling:

> 'I had twa king's bairns living with me in my time and may I never see another.[3]

Pertinent and guaranteed to strike a chord, whichever side you were on, the comment sums up the attitude of lady Drummuir.

Lady Margaret Ogilvy

Lady Margaret Ogilvy was the wife of David Ogilvy, 6th Earl of Airlie. Husband and wife, they were politically and socially compatible, so much so that when the Earl declared his intention to fight with Bonnie Prince Charlie, Lady Margaret was clear – she would go with him.

When in October 1745 Charles Hay, bailee and magistrate of Coupe Angus, read the Declaration of Prince Charles to the assembled populace from the foot of the Mercat Cross in the town, it was a huge shock to the people. Hay had always been considered to be loyal to King

George II but now here he was, committing what was nothing less than a treasonable act.

Then their eyes swivelled to the group clustered around and behind the magistrate. There were several Jacobite personalities from the town but, more significantly, there were the Earl and Lady Ogilvy. They both had their swords drawn and they were pointing them at Charles Hay's back. No wonder Hay was committing treason.

The town of Coupe Angus had a population of just 1500 but it was a strategically important place. To the southwest lay Perth, Dundee was to the southeast. Forfar was situated northeast and the Atholl Mountains spread across the country to the north of the town. Coupe Angus was the perfect gathering place, the gateway to areas like Banff, Angus and Aberdeen where Jacobitism was strongest. Small wonder, then, that the Earl of Ogilvy and his comrades took control of the place.

The scene at Coupe Angus was repeated in many small communities. What made this declaration important was the simple fact that one of the main enforcers was Lady Margaret Ogilvy.

After reading the Declaration from Prince Charles, David and Margaret Ogilvy headed for the home of vintner David Clarke. There, in his study, they found a poster displaying the face of King George. Margaret ripped it from the wall and threw it to the floor. The couple then stamped on it and hurled it out of the open window. When Thomas Eroch, a passer-by, picked up the stained and crumpled poster, Lady Ogilvy called out that the townsfolk should 'Beat that fellow, hard.'

From there Margaret and David Ogilvy joined up with the army of Prince Charles. Margaret Ogilvy accompanied the Jacobite troops when they marched into England and was still with them when they returned in December 1745. She supposedly held her husband's horse at the Battle of Culloden and was taken prisoner at Inverness shortly after the battle ended.

As a woman she might have been considered for a lenient sentence but her ferocity and escapades during the rebellion clearly called for more dramatic consequences. George Miller, Sheriff Deputy for Perthshire, was incensed by all that Lady Margaret had said and done. She must, he declared, be brought to justice:

> This impudent Lady has been using a drawn sword in her delirious Zeal for Hell, France, Rome and the Pretender and

if She and Such as She escape unpunished, Heaven will resent it on us.[4]

David Ogilvy had escaped after the battle, heading for Scandinavia. His wife, however, was left behind and after her arrest, she was duly incarcerated in Edinburgh Castle. As George Miller had hoped, on 15 June 1746 Margaret, Lady Ogilvy, was sentenced to death for acts of treason. Appeals for clemency were refused and she had little option but to sit waiting for the day of execution.

Close friends and relatives, however, had other plans. They centred on Margaret's washerwoman who came regularly to pick up dirty clothes and deliver fresh ones. David Ogilvy's brother and sister were also regular visitors and together with Lady Margaret they persuaded the washerwoman to change clothes with the condemned woman. The only problem was the ungainly walk of the washerwoman. Lady Margaret had to practice for hours to get it right.

Get it right she did and on the evening of 21 November, she walked out of the castle. Originally intending to sail from North Berwick to France, contrary winds kept the ship in harbour and the fugitive had to escape Scotland by road.

At one stage she was, unbelievably, mistaken for no less a person than Bonnie Prince Charlie and was apprehended again. Her travelling companion, the Jacobite Archibald Hart, managed to persuade the soldiers otherwise and after close examination by a woman brought in for the task, Lady Margaret was allowed to go free. It was the end of her wild and dangerous adventures.

Lady Margaret Ogilvy joined her husband in France. They had a child – she went back to Scotland for the birth, determined he would come into the world in her home country – and, in time, were formally allowed back into Britain full-time. They returned happily to Scotland.

Isabel Haldayne, Isabelle Lumsden and Catherine Read

Not really an active Jacobite, Isabel Haldayne still held firm beliefs and by 1745 was a confirmed supporter of Bonnie Prince Charlie. Her husband, Charles Stewart, however, was not sure about the cause. He preferred 'sitting on the fence' as Isabel called it.

Legend declares that she shamed Stewart by taking off her apron and throwing it at him. She declared, loudly, that there was an alternative to him going off to war – 'Stay at home and take care of the house. I will go and command myself.' Charles Stewart promptly jumped down from his fence and joined the Prince's army.

Isabelle Lumsden was another woman who used the force of her personality to garner money for the Prince. She agreed to marry the well-known artist and engraver Robert Strange but only if he pledged his support for Prince Charles. He could do this best, she decided, by using his artistic skills and his talent to create engravings and paintings with a decidedly Jacobite theme. Isabelle then sold these items to wealthy Jacobite ladies to raise money for the cause.

Born in Dundee in 1723, Catherine Read began her career as a painter by producing pastel and pen and ink portraits for local Jacobite families. These were mainly paintings of Jacobite – or assumed Jacobite – ladies and children. Following the defeat of 1745 Catherine and her family fled to France where she came under the influence of the Jacobite painter Robert Strange. She was said to have been in love with the Secretary to Bonnie Prince Charlie, but there is little proof of the statement. However, in Paris she was in regular contact with the Young Pretender and so some sort of relationship was, at least, possible.

Catherine came from a renowned Jacobite family, her uncle John Wedderburn, 5th Earl of Blackness, having been executed for his part in the '45 Rising. Catherine Read later returned to London and became a renowned society painter, working with major Hanoverian figures but never forgetting her Jacobite roots.

Clementina Walkinshaw

Born in 1720, Clementina Walkinshaw came from a Jacobite family but was not directly involved in the '45 Rising. Her connections with Bonnie Prince Charlie came a little later.

Her father, John Walkinshaw, had fought alongside the Old Pretender's troops in 1715 and was captured at the Battle of Sheriffmuir. Imprisoned in Stirling Castle, he managed to escape and fled to Europe. Clementina, his youngest daughter, went with him and was brought up as a devout

Catholic. She returned to Scotland after her father was pardoned and the outbreak of the '45 saw her living with an uncle at Bannockburn.

Clementina had no direct involvement with the Jacobite activities in 1745 but, following Prince Charles' defeat a year later, she followed him into exile in Europe. There must have been some previous contact as long before they became intimate Charles sent her money to help with a debt and then asked her to accompany him to Ghent.

By 1752 Clementina and Charles had moved to Liege and were living together. Clementina was Prince Charles' mistress until 1760, their only child Charlotte being born in 1753.

The relationship between the two, however, was disastrous. By 1753 Prince Charles was already a disillusioned alcoholic.

His violent tempers had not gone, in fact they had grown worse, and he beat Clementina on a regular basis. Finally, Charles' father, the Old Pretender, agreed to her taking refuge in a convent and even gave her an annual sum of money to help her live in some style. Bonnie Prince Charlie never forgave her for what he saw as desertion and refused to pay her anything.

After the death of the Old Pretender in 1766, Clementina was in severe financial difficulties as Charles was still refusing to pay her or their daughter any type of remuneration. Pleading letters and requests fell on deaf ears.

Finally, she was forced to appeal to Charles' brother Cardinal Henry Stuart. He gave her an allowance of 5000 livres on the condition that she made a public statement explaining that she and Prince Charles had never married.

Clementina's final years were a constant search for money and some sort of recognition from Prince Charles. Her daughter Charlotte Stuart was estranged from Charles for several years, a reconciliation taking place not long before the Prince died. Clementina died in Switzerland in 1802.

Mrs Murray of Broughton

Not one of the most renowned of Jacobites but certainly one of the most admired, Mrs Margaret Murray was the wife of John Murray of Broughton, Jacobite Secretary of State during Bonnie Prince Charlie's brief period of power. A beautiful woman who turned heads whenever she appeared in public, she rode beside her husband on many occasions. She rode, it was reported, with an unsheathed sword across her thighs.

The unsheathed sword was a sexually tantalising image, reinforced by the poem or rhyme that was later written about her:

> Ride a cock horse
> To Edinbru Cross
> To see a fine lady
> On a white horse.
>
> (Anonymous)

Margaret and John Murray were later divorced, with claims of adultery being levelled against both parties. Sexual dreams and hidden desires were undoubtedly part of the problem.

Lady Reay

Wife of the 4th Lord Reay, chief of the McKay clan, Lady Reay and her husband were confirmed Jacobites, maintaining their support even after the disaster at Culloden. By 1748, Butcher Cumberland had finished his brutal pursuit of renegade Scotsmen but bands of soldiers were still combing the countryside, searching for stray Jacobite supporters.

As always in the British army, conditions were harsh with physical punishment being a common occurrence for even the most minor offence. When one soldier felt he could take no more, he deserted. Not knowing where he was going, he ran towards the house of Lady Reay in Balnakil and was soon banging at her door, desperate for help. He was exhausted and afraid, with soldiers from his own regiment hot on his trail and even though he was an opponent of the Jacobites, Lady Reay immediately took him in.

When soldiers came pounding at her door, Lady Reay pushed the deserter into a small cupboard at the top of the stairs and took the hunters into the room next door. As the deserter cowered in his cupboard, she entertained his pursuers with alcohol and even went as far as to bring up women from 'downstairs' to take part in an impromptu dance.

The soldiers loved it and, after several hours carousing, went away to continue the hunt, not realising that their quarry had already gone. At her mistress's bidding, one of Lady Reay's servants had hidden him beneath her wide hooped skirt and made slow but steady progress out of the house. A Jacobite giving help to a Hanoverian soldier was an unusual occurrence but it ensured that Lady Reay would go down in history.

Flora MacDonald

The one Jacobite woman everyone seems to know about is Flora MacDonald. Or do they? Her story has been so bowdlerised, so altered and changed - with romantic wishes, fact, fiction and dreams all having been mixed together in a mishmash of false history - that much of the reality has been lost or misplaced. So, what do we really know about the Scottish heroine?

Flora was born in 1722 on the island of South Uist. Her father, a tacksman, died when she was just two years old and the young girl found herself being looked after by her father's cousin, Sir Alexander MacDonald, and his wife Margaret. As a consequence of this 'adoption', she maintained a rather privileged life style, was well educated and was certainly not the meek, mild and simple country girl of legend.

Being the daughter of a tacksman Flora had been born into a position of some significance. Tacksmen were, effectively, minor gentry in Scottish society, renting land from landowners and then sub-letting portions of it to other, lesser tenants. It was a position or role that was to disappear as the later Clearances began to bite but when she was young Flora MacDonald enjoyed the significance of her position.

After her husband's death Flora's mother married again, this time to Hugh MacDonald, another tacksman and a member of what can be regarded as the minor gentry of the Hebrides. The MacDonalds of the islands were split in their support for Prince Charles and King George but even those like Hugh, at first glimpse an out-and-out Hanoverian, were not above turning a blind eye when it came to helping the Prince in his hour of difficulty and contributing to the effort of getting him out of the country.

The popularity of Flora MacDonald as a Scottish woman of note owes much of its significance to the need for a romantic heroine in the face of the Jacobite defeat. The young girl who helped Bonnie Prince Charlie to escape the clutches of the Hanoverian government was the perfect figure to take and use. She did what she felt she had to do, others embellished the legend and developed the tales about her character and actions.

James Boswell and Dr Samuel Johnson met Flora during their trip through the Highlands and islands of Scotland in 1773, nearly thirty years after her escapade with Bonnie Prince Charlie. Boswell recorded his first meeting with her:

> There was a comfortable parlour with a good fire, and a dram went round. By and by supper was served, at which there appeared the lady of the house, the celebrated Miss Flora MacDonald. She is a little woman, of a genteel appearance, and uncommonly mild and well bred.[5]

The irascible Dr Johnson also liked and admired Flora, that in itself being a complement to her intelligence, her good manners and her genteel behaviour. There were many learned and famous members of society, celebrities that Johnson encountered during his life, who did not receive anything like his response to Flora MacDonald. Put simply, he was clearly infatuated with her.

Flora was not above 'playing the game' with the good Dr Johnson. Just as she had done with her interrogators many years before, she gave him exactly what his self-interested personality required. She was modest about her part in Prince Charles' escape and handled Johnson perfectly, smoothing his ego and pandering to his vision of himself:

> Here I had the honour of saluting the far-famed Miss Flora Macdonald, who conducted the Prince through the English forces from the island of Lewes, and when she came to Skye dined with the English officers. She must then have been a young lady, she is now not old, of a pleasing person (sic) and elegant behaviour. She told me that she thought herself honoured by my visit, and I am sure that whatever regard she bestowed on me, was liberally repaid.[6]

Not an out-and-out Jacobite, Flora nevertheless had a degree of sympathy with the Stuart cause, albeit a very small one. Even so, it was not enthusiasm for the Jacobites that made her take on the difficult and dangerous task of helping Charles Edward Stuart to escape. As she later told Frederick, Prince of Wales when she was received by him in London, she would have done the same for him if he had needed help.

Flora's part in the story came five months after the Jacobite defeat at Culloden. Prince Charles had spent that time as a fugitive with a price on his head, hundreds of Hanoverian troops searching the heather and the farmsteads for a glimpse of the fleeing Prince. The Royal Navy scoured the seas and maintained a firm blockade of the Scottish coast but Charles remained on the run.

There were many near misses, Hanoverian soldiers sometimes failing by minutes to catch him. The hunt was at its peak in the early summer of 1746 and it was clear that government troops would inevitably lay hands on him if he did not manage to get out of Scotland soon. Moving quickly but surreptitiously, Charles and his companions headed doggedly west, towards the islands off the Scottish coast, hoping to find a ship to take them back to France.

Prince Charles had been helped by many people during his time as a fugitive, notably women like Catriona Graham who provided him with 'highland cloths,' clothing that would help disguise him and be more hard-wearing than his princely garb. In Graham's case, it cost her dearly. Shortly after the Prince had left her house, refreshed and newly clothed, the place was ransacked and then burned by Captain Fergusson, one of the most notorious Jacobite hunters of the time.[7]

Now, when the Prince appeared on South Uist, Hugh MacDonald realised he had to get him away, double quick. Captain Ferguson and his colleague Captain Scott, both hated and feared Hanoverians, had moved their search for renegade Jacobites to the Hebrides. Hugh MacDonald knew that they would not hesitate to send their troops sweeping like wildfire through the islands if they felt there was a chance of capturing their quarry.

Prince Charles was a dangerous man to have on his hands and MacDonald realised that, for the safety of the man himself as well as the islanders, he had to be moved out of the country. And for that, MacDonald turned to his step daughter Flora.

The plan was simple enough. Flora, who had been sent to an isolated bothy on South Uist in order to oversee the family flock of sheep – an attempt to create an alibi if ever there was one – would conduct Bonnie Prince Charlie by boat to the outer islands where he might find a ship.

The Prince would be disguised as a woman. Special female clothing to allow for his height and bulk was prepared – the task of Catriona Graham.

Smuggling out the Prince was dangerous and it put the young Flora at very great risk but it was a logical move, particularly with the Prince travelling in the guise of a woman. Ferguson and Scott would be looking for men, not a pair of women.

To begin with Flora was unwilling and afraid. There were so many ways the plan could go wrong, everything from trigger-happy soldiers to the wild tide race between the islands, and if she was caught Flora knew there would be no mercy from the government. She was also afraid for her reputation, spending time alone with a rake like Prince Charles. It took a personal request from the Prince but, at last, Flora reluctantly agreed.[8]

Late at night towards the end of June Prince Charles and a handful of comrades appeared at Flora's door. The Prince quickly donned the clothes prepared for him and when dressed as Betty Burke, maid or servant to Flora, they set off. Passports and travel documents in the names of Flora MacDonald and Betty Burke had been provided by Hugh MacDonald.

The 'two women' moved to the island of Benbecula where, on 27 June, they picked up a boat for the final stage of the journey. Contrary to legend – and the line from *The Skye Boat Song* – there were no soldiers standing on the shore, afraid to follow the fugitives; the weather and the water were dangerous enough on their own.

The story of Flora MacDonald shielding, guiding and keeping watch over the Prince during the wild crossing to Skye is another piece of fiction. Flora fell asleep and woke to find Charles with his hands and arms above her head, protecting her from the feet of the boatmen as they hurried about the decking on their duties.

Arriving safely on Skye, on 1 July the Prince and the Scottish heroine parted, he to the isle of Ramsay, she back the way she had come. They never met again. It had been a tumultuous few weeks, Flora giving the Prince the rough edge of her tongue on several occasions when his natural arrogance and superiority came out. He was supposed to be a woman, a maid at that – so, act like one!

Bonnie Prince Charlie was the Young Pretender right enough but he was no actor. To be fair to him, his posture, his bearing, everything he had been trained in all of his life, were against him. As one genuine maid commented after seeing him walk past 'I have never seen such a tall, impudent jaund in all my life. See what long strides she takes.'

Prince Charles spent some time on the island but by the end of the summer, he was on board ship, leaving Scotland on 19 September bound for exile in France and Italy. Flora was not so lucky. Somebody talked, giving away her part in the escape, and she was duly arrested.

She spent a year in various prison environments – a prison ship in Leith Roads and a cell in the Tower of London being just two of them. She was taken to London by ship, a hazardous journey at the best of times. Some of the prison transports suffered fifty to sixty per-cent fatalities but Flora was lucky and spared the worst indignities. Her trip south on the *Bridgewater* may not have been first-class travel but she made the trip uninjured.

Given enormous latitude in her captivity, Flora MacDonald assumed celebrity status almost from the beginning. She received a constant stream of visitors and was even allowed freedom to leave prison in the Tower of London and visit people outside.

Such freedom had begun in the early days of her captivity when the captain of the prison ship *HMS Bridgewater*, yet another man to fall under the spell of her charms, gave her the run of his ship. Once ensconced in the Tower the 'careful' handling of Flora MacDonald continued.

Free to walk more or less where she wanted, to dine with Jacobite and Hanoverian supporters alike, there were also other huge benefits suddenly available for the Scottish heroine. Money now became no object as influential people made collections for her, Frederick, Prince of Wales being one of the contributors. Flora accepted the money and gifts with the gracious charm she had shown throughout her adventures.

Interrogated and questioned ad nauseum, Flora did give the names of some Jacobite supporters, in all probability names that were already known to the interrogators. However, she was pleasant and seemingly honest in her answers to questions and charmed her captors in a way that few Jacobites ever managed to do. Arrogance and aggression had never been in her nature and she was not going to change her personality now.

The result was that Flora was herself treated with respect and more than a little admiration. Playing the political game (large and small 'p') clearly came easily to her. If the attitude of most captured Jacobites,

Jacobite women in particular, was one of barely concealed hostility and aggression, Flora MacDonald came from the opposite pole.

Never brought to trial, Flora MacDonald was released under the terms of an amnesty of July 1747. Surprisingly, she did not immediately return to the Hebrides. She had grown used to the life of a celebrity and headed for Edinburgh instead. It was not long before she was back in London, revelling in the balls and coffee houses, enjoying the adulation and heroic status she had been given. It took time but eventually, she returned to the islands. And yet she was not really happy there.

Legend had already declared Flora MacDonald a hero but there were many in Scotland who questioned her motives and her actions. Captain Ferguson, for one, tried hard to imply there were sexual relations between the Prince and Flora. There was no evidence and the allegation dissolved into unrealistic rumour.

Others resented the ease with which Flora had been treated when many Jacobite supporters, men and women alike, had endured much harder fates. Why should others suffer, the hardcore Stuart supporters asked, when she was being wined, dined and having her portrait painted by renowned artists like Richard Wilson and Allan Ramsey. They were not just ordinary paintings, many noted, but portraits which showed Flora in traditional Scottish dress.

As all Scots knew only too well, the 1747 Act of Proscription had outlawed the tartan, the wearing of kilts and even use of the bagpipes which, according to the Hanoverian government were deemed an instrument of war! Quite what Flora made of that last ruling against bagpipes has not been recorded for posterity.

It all made for very unpleasant listening, however. There are no records or reports of Flora MacDonald being unduly upset by the debate. She was, after all, the woman who had braved the elements and the Hanoverians in order to get Bonnie Prince Charlie to safety. She was not lacking in courage but the opposition to her and her actions must have been unsettling.

As with many people in post-Jacobite Scotland, Flora and her new husband Allan MacDonald soon ran into money problems. In an effort to circumvent these difficulties, they emigrated to America, taking ship from the Clyde and settling in North Carolina where they acquired land and settled down to the life of genteel farming.

They were doing well until the American War of Independence erupted. Amazingly, Allan MacDonald declared for the British crown, even raising a regiment of soldiers to fight against the rebels. He had always been something of a supporter of the Hanoverians; Flora had never been a Jacobite so perhaps the move was not so surprising after all.

Victory for the American colonists ruined the holdings and prospects of the MacDonald family and they duly returned to the Hebrides. Despite the loss of two of her children and a husband who never really understood her, Flora settled down to life on the islands of Scotland. Her final years were not easy, ill health dogging her to the end.

She died on Skye in 1790. Dr Johnson, his enchantment never fading, wrote the words for the inscription on her memorial in Kilmuir Cemetery:

> Flora MacDonald. Preserver of Charles Edward Stuart. Her name will be mentioned in history and if courage and loyalty be still virtues, mentioned with honour.[9]

Enchantment, infatuation, whatever it was, Dr Johnson's words provided a fitting epitaph for the woman who remains, even now nearly 300 years after the Jacobite defeat at Culloden, a significant Scottish heroine.

Lady Clan

Lady Clanranald, the determined and irascible wife of Lord Clanranald, Old Clanranald as he was known, was both practical and skilled with a needle. She was the chief dressmaker who prepared the costume for Betty Burke during Prince Charles' escape. She also provided him, along with Flora MacDonald and the boat crew, with bread and milk to sustain them on their trip.

Arrested by government forces when it became clear that the Prince had escaped, she and her husband were transported to London where they were kept in separate confinement for many months. Lady Clan, however, found herself with little to do except sit and worry about her children back in Scotland. As a result, she suffered a mental breakdown, went 'raving mad' as one man described her.

She was ordered to be sent to Bedlam but Mrs Money, proprietor of the Messenger House where she had been lodged, refused to move her. The order was discretely ignored.

Chapter Eleven

The Clearances and More

The war was over, Prince Charles was safely away over 'the friendly main', but that was not the end of the affair. In many respects, the worst was yet to come.

The day after Culloden, Prince Charles paused in his flight to issue an order to those of his troops who remained under arms. Many of his most substantial supporters and followers had found security at places such as the Ruthven Barracks where over 1000 clansmen were gathered, waiting for the Prince's orders.

Those orders, when they came, were for them to 'seek their own safety' and disband. Some did exactly that. Others turned their faces and their weapons in the opposite direction and became outlaws, raiding cattle and operating as a kind of underground resistance or Fifth Column. In the best traditions of Rob Roy, Robin Hood, Owain Glyndwr and other notable bandits they also offered protection to the farmers and tenants of an increasingly vulnerable community. Perhaps the best portrayal of these times and of the people involved can be found not in the history books but in Walter Scott's fictional works like *Waverley*, *Redgauntlet* and *Rob Roy*:

> Ye hae still mony hundreds and thousands o' lang-legged Highland gillies that will neither work nor want, and maun gang thigging and soring (begging) about on their acquaintance- - - And mair especially, mony hundreds o' them come down to the borders of the low country where there's gear to grip, and live by stealing, reiving, lifting cows, and the like depredations.[1]

When soldiers did surrender their arms, the results were not always favourable. After a government promise of six weeks freedom from punishment, a number of Highlanders duly turned themselves in at

Fort William. Their reward was to be drowned in a salmon net set up by the infamous Captain Scott. Small wonder then that many chose to fight on, taking to the hills which they knew and loved but which most of the redcoat soldiers did not.

There were many others who would not trust the security of the caves and heather-clad hills. These men went abroad to join the Irish Brigade or one of the numerous Scottish regiments then serving the French, units such as the Ecossaise Royales.

It was the start of a Scottish tradition, clansmen enlisting in one or other of the various armies of powerful nations – not least Britain. The Clearances and the de-population of the Highlands had seriously damaged the traditional Scottish way of life. Farming and crofting might have been out but fighting was not, even if it was for the British army. Life in the army was not easy with harsh discipline and postings to hot and humid countries that exhausted the fittest of men but for many Scots it was, until 1914-18, one sure way of finding security and value.

An attempt to create a united front was made in May 1746 when a gathering of the clansmen resulted in an agreement to fight on and to only lay down their arms when all of the clan chiefs gave the order. Despite the pledges and, later that year, a relatively small gathering of some 600 clansmen in the northern Highlands, nothing came of the decision to fight as an entity. That summer, there were insurrections in areas like Argyll but these were isolated incidents which caused little real bother to the Hanoverian government.

Butcher Cumberland – or Sweet William as the Hanoverians called him – was determined to obliterate the danger of any future Jacobite challenge to the crown. He was, after all, a significant representative of the Hanoverian dynasty and if the Hanoverians lost power, then so too did he. On the other hand, if the Hanoverians went from strength to strength, he would accompany them on their journey. It was a simple equation, one that Cumberland would understand and win, one that the Jacobites would lose.

By now Cumberland had nearly 13,000 government troops under his command. He planned his movements carefully and soon had them deployed across the whole of Scotland. It was the start of a dictatorial and draconian period of control, one that saw murder and mayhem, destruction and deprivation in almost every part of the country.

Cumberland's initial response was a knee-jerk reaction that, to begin with, came largely from anger. But that reaction was soon developed into a clearly thought-out policy, firstly from Cumberland himself and then from the Hanoverian government. Destroying the Jacobites was only part of the solution. Destroying the emotions and the forces that drove them was a considerably more targeted approach.

So, how to begin? If they couldn't get their hands on the Young Pretender, the Hanoverians felt, they could certainly do their best to destroy support for the man and all he stood for. In Butcher Cumberland, they had the ideal man to start the job.

It was not simply a personal viewpoint but Cumberland's brutal beliefs and actions in the immediate aftermath of his victory at Culloden quickly became accepted policy by the Whig politicians back in London. Not since the working out of the Norman Conquest in the years after 1066 had such a destructive killing spree been government sponsored and, worst of all, government-implemented.

Regardless of Cumberland's immediate actions after Culloden, his and the Hanoverian/Whig responses were largely unexpected by the Scots. The rising of 1715 had led to only very limited repercussions from the victorious Hanoverian government, just half a dozen executions and a number of men exiled and attainted. Most of the attainted exiles were later returned to their homes and estates with, on the surface at least, everything forgiven.

The aftermath of the '45 was altogether different and that was, initially, thanks to Cumberland. He began his campaign by highlighting and pursuing all those with Jacobite sympathies but it became quickly apparent that most of the major rebels had already foreseen their danger and escaped to France, to the Netherlands and to other more welcoming countries.

Cumberland and his lackies were forced to search for 'smaller fry'. As a result, relatively minor Scottish participants and aristocrats like Lord Lovat and Lord Kilmarnock were apprehended and executed before the Butcher Cumberland's officers and officials moved on to men of the lower social order:

> Altogether there were 120 executions, over a hundred deaths in prison, and over 1000 banishments and transportations. In Scotland Cumberland instituted the reign of terror that has made his name a byword for savagery.[2]

Cumberland began his work by instigating a period of martial law. In itself martial law was something of a nuisance but it was not normally a particularly onerous punishment. However, this was a very individual appreciation of the time-honoured military practice. Cumberland had no intention of simply implementing curfews or of policing the streets with soldiers. He would be proactive across the whole of Scotland and view all of its people as his targets.

What he did was to give his troops free rein to pillage their way across the Highlands and Lowlands. Houses were looted and sacked, barns and property were burned, women and men apprehended and beaten to a pulp. Women were even raped, on the high roads and in the streets of the towns. The more mayhem the better.

For the haughty Duke of Cumberland, this was a time of retribution and a levelling of old scores. It was also financially rewarding as much of the looted possessions and property did not remain with the rank-and-file soldiers but found its way into the ownership of the officers and aristocrats in Cumberland's army.

Cumberland had no qualms or regrets about what he was doing. Scotland, he insisted, was a vile spot, one that might 'still be the ruin of this island and our family'.[3] That was the key to his behaviour, the need to protect the royal family from ruin.

It was a difficult and dangerous few months for the Scots and when Butcher Cumberland had done his worst it was time for the Hanoverian government to take over.

Everything the government did, all the laws they instigated and enforced, were designed to humiliate the Scottish people and destroy their culture. They were only marginally less brutal and oppressive than soldier's musket butts beating on the cottage doors or the boots of Cumberland's 'warriors' smashing against the windows of cottages across the land. And unlike a beating or a wounding, the laws and rulings were long-lasting in the extreme.

In order to make everything legally acceptable, two Acts of Parliament, the Vesting and Annexing Acts, ensured that all forfeited property would remain firmly grasped in the sticky palms of the Hanoverian government and its officers. It was hardly in keeping with the 1707 Act of Union and certainly not the time to be a Scottish house holder or tenant farmer.

The Jacobites may have been beaten on the battlefield but their enthusiasm and desire for freedom had not been crushed. Imprisonment whilst awaiting trial – in itself a harsh enough punishment – was the initial fate of many Jacobite men and women.

As it turned out, however, the prisons and jails were not ready for such an influx of prisoners. Guards were either old and infirm or disinterested in keeping prisoners secure. In some cases, the jailers even had Jacobite sympathies and were willing, for a few pounds, to turn their backs and close their eyes. Doors and locks were antiquated, windows were broken and left open to the world. As a result, escape, especially for those waiting for execution, became a logical pattern of behaviour.

With flight or disappearance from custody becoming more and more common, security had to be tightened in all of the British jails. It was efficiently and effectively done. In the first few months after the Battle of Culloden there had been fifty-eight successful escapes, most of them from Scottish prisons. By 1747, after a long period of draconian regulations and the implementation of rules that would have pleased the Duke of Cumberland, that figure had dropped to just one.

Once out of prison, legally or by escape, Jacobites were faced with a dilemma. What to do next? Many of them chose to abandon soldiering, to leave their homeland and make new and more peaceful futures for themselves overseas.

Jacobite exiles spread their tentacles widely, making homes for their families in countries like America, Canada, New Zealand and Australia. Away from the ever-present hand of Butcher Cumberland and the menace of the Hanoverian government, they excelled in professions like banking, farming, military service and politics. The sad part of their achievements was that they had to leave their homeland in order to find such success.

And the Jacobite women? Strange as it might seem in the wake of the Puritan tightrope of the 1650s and the coming of their diametrically opposed successors – people such as Charles II and his courtiers – the eighteenth century was something of a permissive age. And that made for some very strange bedfellows, creating relationships that went far beyond the boudoirs of the time.

Royal mistresses and figures like Sarah Churchill, wife of the Duke of Marlborough, wielded amazing amounts of influence. Small wonder, then, that on many occasions people asked who actually ruled Britain,

Sarah Churchill or Queen Anne? It was an interesting and debatable point – and the questioners' tongues were not always in their cheeks!

Sarah Churchill was no Jacobite, her husband having absconded from the service of James II in 1688, before the King's army could face up to William of Orange. And she was not interested in the Queen sexually. Her interest and influence were on the side of the Hanoverians who controlled the future of the *nouveau riche* Sarah and her family.

In their own way, Jacobite women were as influential as Sarah Churchill, albeit from a different corner of the stage. And they continued to wield that influence up to the final days of the movement.

Jacobitism had long offered a place and a point of refuge for women, particularly those who had no desire to become involved in the drab and unfulfilling marriages that were typical of the upper classes in those days.

Such marriages were not only the normal course of life for women of the supposedly privileged elite, they were the only way to avoid being looked down upon by luckier individuals. Social snubs and the pointing fingers of critics directed at old maidens left on the shelf were to be avoided at all costs.

Consequently, many women found themselves stuck on the horns of a dilemma. Should they remain single and be sneered at by all and sundry? Or was it better to subside into an existence where the most taxing event of the week was to check that the kitchen staff were not fiddling the family food bill? There had to be an alternative:

> Women and Jacobitism could come together in a mutual embrace of the outsiders and the marginalised. Both were minorities, and each could find uses in the other ... Women could use their ingenuity as secret agents, couriers and lovers to help the Jacobite cause.[4]

Long before the demise of Bonnie Prince Charlie and even after he was safely back in France, women continued to be significant players in the ranks of Jacobite exiles. Often their involvement was in a subliminal rather than an active way. Three of the most notable examples of Jacobite women were the impressive and beautiful Oglethorpe sisters.

The Oglethorpes came, originally, from Surrey but the girls accompanied their parents, who were fervent Jacobites, when they followed James II into exile in 1688. Over the next decade, Fanny and Anne made regular appearances at James' court outside Paris, charming the exiled Jacobites and the French courtiers. At one stage Fanny was even thought to be the mistress of the exiled monarch. She featured in exactly that role as a character in *Henry Esmond*, the novel by William Makepeace Thackeray but it is hard to know which came first, the rumour or the novel.

The third Oglethorpe girl was Eleanor. She was just a baby when the Glorious Revolution exiled her and her family to France and so she grew up in the Jacobite court, surrounded by elegance, romance and not a little subterfuge.

A beautiful and self-possessed woman, after several years at Germain-en-Laye Eleanor married the Marquis de Mezieres, himself a reasonably well-off soldier and nobleman. She then made a fortune by 'selling short' – disposing of shares when they were at their height and before their price plummeted - during the so-called Mississippi Bubble of 1720.

With her money and good looks, Eleanor now stood at the pinnacle of French nobility, feted and applauded whenever she appeared in public. And from that lofty position she used everything in her power to lobby for the Jacobites.

It is difficult to know how effective her lobbying actually was but continued French support for the Old and Young Pretenders seems to indicate that to the end of her long life, she remained a force to be reckoned with in the courts of the French kings.

Eleanor Oglethorpe and her sisters were such significant figures in the coterie surrounding James and his courtiers that they were often spoken about in the same breath as the more famous Olive Trant. In a letter detailing some of the activities of the Jacobite court at Germain-en-Laye, Henry St John, the 1st Viscount Bolingbroke, foreign minister for the Old Pretender, produced the following simple but telling lines:

> No sex was excluded from the ministry. Fanny Oglethorpe, whom you have seen in England, kept her corner in it, and Olive Trant was the great wheel of our machine.[5]

Bolingbroke's letters were later published in book form but only after his death. In an age of elegant writing, they remain fluent and revealing.

He certainly understood and appreciated the presence of women like the Oglethorpe and Trant sisters.

James, always a sucker for a pretty face, was charmed by Olive Trant, calling her 'the young nymph'. She was one of three daughters to Sir Patrick Trant, a less-than-honest lawyer from County Dublin, who had been absolved of his many crimes and debts when James II became King of England in 1685. Chief amongst these was the embezzlement of £10,000 from the widow of Sir William Stapleton but there were others, many others.

The three Trant sisters were sent to Paris to be educated by the famous Blue Nuns of the city. Following the Glorious Revolution of 1688, the sisters were joined in France by their parents. The exile was, for the sisters at least, a very genteel affair. For their father, it was a somewhat more military or martial time.

Sir Patrick served with James II during his brief invasion of Ireland in 1689 and fought alongside him at the Battle of the Boyne. Criminal he may have been but Sir Patrick was no coward so that when James sent him on a desperate mission that took him away from the battlefield he was not best pleased. Nevertheless, he did as he was directed and left the field.

James was not trying to keep Sir Patrick safe. With things clearly going badly for his troops, James took a practical view of the situation. He had tried to do too much, too soon.

Sir Patrick was sent by the former King to appropriate a ship in order to take them both away from Ireland and get them back to France. As a result, Sir Patrick was declared a traitor by William of Orange, not for helping the exiled monarch by fighting in battle but for the heinous crime of helping him to escape. It was, William of Orange declared, an act of High Treason.

As she grew older Olive Trant became totally infatuated by the grandeur and the glory of the courts at Germain-en-Laye and at Versailles. She eventually married the wealthy Frederic-Jules, Prince of Auvergne, in the process becoming the Princess of Auvergne.

Rich at last, to a level beyond even her father's wildest dreams, Olive managed to use her money and her charms to keep the Jacobite flag flying high in the halls of the French monarchs and noblemen.

* * *

The Highland Clearances, the politically motivated depredation of Scotland and its people, were carried out in two carefully planned phases lasting from approximately 1750 until the mid-1850s. In both phases, the British government was only too conscious of the effect of the Clearances on the Scottish people.

Conscious of it, yes, but government motives were far from charitable. They tried hard to cloak the effects of what they termed 'removals' – the name Clearances was not used until 1843, the middle of the nineteenth century – as methods of improving life on the crofts and farms. In fact, the Clearances had nothing whatsoever to do with improving the lot of Scottish people.

On the contrary, the Clearances were an attempt at breaking down the traditional clan system through the implementation of what the Scots soon saw as 'foreign' procedures and beliefs. It was a re-drawing or re-modelling of the population in the image of English Whig ideals and thereby keeping Scotland firmly underfoot. As a result, within two or three decades and in the wake of a massive de-population of the countryside, old Scotland effectively died.

Phase One began soon after Culloden, lasting until 1815, and disguised itself under the shrouding veil of agricultural improvement and the prevention of total economic collapse. There was a small element of truth in the claim, albeit secondary and of minor importance. Put simply, landlords had to increase their income or face potential bankruptcy. It began, perhaps inevitably, with the implementation of enclosures, a practice which appealed to the large land owners but to almost nobody else.

Clan leaders, self-interested in the extreme, saw the writing on the wall. People like the chief of the Clan Campbell, holding huge estates in the Highlands, was the Duke of Argyll, a title duly passed on to members of his family. He embraced the enclosures and, inevitably, other clan chiefs followed suit as this new style of farming and cultivation gave them the opportunity and the money to change their ways of life.

The large open fields which tenant farmers had for many years used for communal grazing were now fenced in and turned over to crop growing and the mixed pastoral farming of cattle and sheep. Higher rents were also charged. Without consultation or discussion, it effectively reduced tenant farmers to the role of simple crofters.

Clan chiefs became little more than commercial landlords but the clan members, schooled and brought up with the inalienable right to rent land in clan territory, continued to hold on to the past, to the age-old system of duthches as the process was termed. They could not understand and certainly did not agree with the new arrangements.

The system might have put money into the pockets of the land owners but it caused huge resentment amongst the tenant farmers and crofters. Many tenants were unable to afford the higher rents and were forced to move to one of the big cities like Glasgow where they tried to make a living in one of the new manufacturing industries. Others simply starved.

The enclosure system meant that rich landowners got richer as they realised there was more money to be made in raising sheep than in any of the traditional methods of farming. The old system had worked reasonably well but there had been little interest in improving the land through procedures like crop rotation. And, of course, destruction of the 'old ways' was one of the first nails in the coffin of rebellious clansmen.

Flocks of sheep might need just one or two men to look after them, that was all, meaning that there was no longer any need to rent out land to the crofters. The shepherds were usually brought in from other parts of the country, denying local crofters even that chance of jobs. The 'rum rig' system of allocating plots of land to crofters on an annual basis died out very quickly and Sottish labourers, the clansmen of old, were left with no way of earning even the barest of livings.

Phase Two, which ran from 1815 and continued until the middle years of the century, had to deal with overcrowding in the cities and industrial areas, problems that had been caused by the implementation of Phase One. Displaced tenant farmers had moved from their traditional homes and farms into urban centres or towns where, if they were lucky, they were able to find jobs in industries like fishing and quarrying.

Reliance on the available industries put too many eggs in too few baskets. The kelp industry, for example, was one that suffered from over production.

Kelp or seaweed was gathered from the seashore and used in the making of glass and soap, a process that required large numbers of workers. However, from 1810 onwards the price of kelp began to fall.

In 1823 it was fetching £9 a ton but five years later that price had dropped to just over £3 a ton. Kelp farming had become too expensive. It was no longer viable, at least not in the form that the Scots knew and understood.

Wool prices also dropped, meaning that landlords had less disposable income and that many factories closed their doors. Many of the wool workers, like those employed gathering kelp, were now out of a job.

Things were not helped by famines such as the Highland Potato Famine of 1846-1856 which saw a third of the population of western Scotland either dead or forced to emigrate. The potato blight was repeated in Ireland and other rural areas and was devastating in its effect, literally wiping out what had become part of the staple diet of the people.

The collapse of many traditional industries left people with no way of supporting themselves. They had to look elsewhere for wages and a living. Assisted passages, the fares sometimes even paid by landlords, saw hundreds of Scots move abroad in an attempt to find better living conditions. It has been estimated that 16,000 men, women and children left Scotland for new lives in America and Canada in this period.

The Scots, like the Irish, never forgot their homeland. But they did not grieve for it in the way that the Irish refugees were to do. The Scots adopted a more philosophical and pragmatic approach to their exile.

Perhaps that pragmatism was in their character, perhaps defeat in the '15 and '45 risings had destroyed their belief in any real form of just reward. Perhaps, more than anything else, by leaving Scotland as a family, by emigrating and surviving as a strong unit, they had no need to live on dreams and desires. There was room and time for that in the Jacobite ballads.

The idea of assisted passages to new countries was no act of generosity. It was a case of go voluntarily or we will force you off the land, a practical but draconian method of removing crofters and workers from the land where they could no longer earn a living. For the landlords, emigration meant one less problem to deal with!

More than anything, however, the Clearances and their after-effects also meant the end of the traditional Scottish clan life. Clan members had always believed in adherence to the family of the clan and to the clan chief. That was the basis of the whole Scottish clan system, that adherence and loyalty which went both ways, from the clansmen up and from the clan chiefs down. It had survived centuries of war and disaster. Not anymore.

The changes and the Clearances meant that clan chiefs were no longer the patriarchs of their people, they were simply commercial landlords out to make money, in charge of what might easily be termed an early example of ethnic cleansing.

It was a difficult time for Scotland and the Scots, the Clearances in the Highlands and on the islands bringing very little stability. Serious riots broke out in many parts of Scotland in the early years of the nineteenth century, eye witness accounts from 1813 recording over 250 houses and farms ablaze in one district alone.[6]

The end of the Clearances in the middle years of the nineteenth century might have been a blessing in disguise but it left behind an empty hole in the centre of Scottish society. Perhaps more significantly, it left a bitterly hurt and damaged people. They were not alone but the Clearances had helped to create a resentment that has never yet gone totally away.

Chapter Twelve

Literary Jacobite Women and Men

Defeat at Culloden, the implementation of Highland Clearances, the destruction of much of Scottish culture and society, repeated attempts by the Hanoverian government in London to wipe out their way of life, it was as if war had been declared on Scottish society. And the attacks – because that was what they were – had left the Scots with only one way to go; full tilt into the dream world of romance. This in turn, led to the sad but lasting emotion of longing for things from the past. Unlike so much else, Scottish romanticism was one of the few things to grow and develop in these years.

The Scots had always had a sentimental side to their character, as shown by the profusion of Jacobite songs written during the long wait between the Old Pretender's invasion of 1715 and the coming of Bonnie Prince Charlie thirty years later. But that was nothing compared to the wave of romanticism that erupted in the late eighteenth and early nineteenth centuries. It was something that began with the Culloden defeat and was still going strong over a hundred years later. Arguably, it continues even today.

That popularity does not necessarily equate with quality. An overfill of sentiment has ruined many a good poem but where that emotion is carefully handled it can touch at the heart strings of even the most embittered and disinterested of readers. And with the best of the Scottish Jacobite-inspired poems and songs that was exactly what happened.

One of the first exponents of this romanticism was the poet and song writer Carolina Oliphant, otherwise known as Lady Nairne. The fourth child of Laurence Oliphant, Laird of Gask, and Margaret Robertson, Carolina was born in 1766, twenty years after the Battle of Culloden.

Despite the defeat, Carolina's family remained strong Jacobite supporters and in the wake of the battle, as repercussions mounted in fury, they found themselves labelled as traitors. Eventually, they were forced into exile, away from their homeland.

The family returned from France in 1764, having been pardoned and given back their estates. It was just two years before Carolina was born. It had been an empty, hollow time but the brief period of exile had done nothing to lessen the extent of Jacobite fury in their hearts.

Brought up to venerate the Jacobite cause, Carolina and her sisters were determined to make a stand. They did it with their prayer books where the names of the Hanoverian monarchs were listed – a common enough process in the Hanoverian age. With adolescent delight, the girls used slips of white paper to cover the names of the Hanoverian kings and queens, replacing them with the names, dates and titles of the exiled Stuarts. Such a practice was hardly revolutionary but it was still regarded as a treasonable offence by members of the Hanoverian government.

Childhood was a genteel and relaxed upbringing with Carolina becoming expert in painting, drawing and, in particular, in music and verse. She married William Murray, the 5th Lord Nairne in 1824, the marriage lasting just a few years before ending with William's untimely death.

After her husband's early death Carolina lived for a while in Ireland, before spending some time travelling on the continent. She was, however, at her happiest in her native land and soon returned to Scotland.

She had begun writing seriously in 1792, working as a poet rather than a musician. Many of her compositions were set to traditional Scottish airs, already known and loved by the people. It was a successful format and soon her efforts were being published and sung all over the country. The most famous of her compositions include *Will Ye No' Come Back Again, Charlie is My Darling, The Rowan Tree* and *Wi' a Hundred Pipers*. Popular at the time, they have since been sung and recorded by artists as varied as Kenneth McKellar, the Irish folk band The Clancy Brothers and legendary Scottish singer Ewan McCall.

A contemporary of Robert Burns, Carolina published anonymously for many years, fearing that her work would not be taken seriously if people realised it had been written by a woman. For a while she wrote under the pen name of Mrs Bogan of Bogan but, realising this was too obvious she soon assumed the gender-neutral name, title or appellation of BB. Sometimes, like most ballad writers of the time, she provided her work with no attribution at all.

Always a woman of humour and decorum, Carolina even kept her creative talent hidden from her husband, although she did confide in several of her female companions. When asked if William knew of her compositions and her musical career she smiled and replied, simply 'I have not told Nairne lest he blabs.'[1]

The downside to this desire for anonymity was that her work was sometimes confused with that of Robbie Burns. Carolina, however, wrote in the spirit of romance, her vision of Scotland and the Jacobites centring on the sadness of what had gone and would not now return. Burns had a different intent with his poetry.

Robert Burns has long been regarded as the pioneer of the romantic movement and there is no doubt that he and his work provided inspiration for the creators or founders of liberalism, even the long distant dream of socialism, in the late nineteenth century. Unashamedly liberal in attitude, he has also been hugely influential as far as other creative artists are concerned.

Both Bob Dylan and Michael Jackson have gone on record, listing him as one of their great influences. Dylan has cited *A Red, Red Rose* as a major motivator for much of his song writing while Jackson claimed that *Tam O'Shanter* was the impetus behind his song *Thriller* and the longer, more in-depth album of the same name.

There is no doubt about the place of Burns in the pantheon of great poets. However, as far as the Jacobite swing towards pure romanticism is concerned he will have to take second place to people like Carolina Oliphant.

Burns was born just south of Ayr in 1759. He came from a farming family and did in fact spend some years as a farmer himself. His real interest, however, was in writing, producing work in the Scottish idiom and dialect and in straightforward English. His style of writing was spontaneous, direct and filled with sincerity.

As a man of his time, Burns was himself influenced by Radicalism and Republicanism, meaning that he wrote about diverse issues such as inequalities, gender roles and cultural identity. When the mood took him, he was also capable of producing comic poetry and verse that was both funny and cutting.

Renowned for his intemperance and womanising, Burns often referred to his 'blue devilism'. He meant the severe bouts of depression from which he suffered and one theory is that he was a manic depressive. If that is true – and it is an allegation that has never been proved one way or the other – it may account for his inability to fully and wholeheartedly romanticise the Jacobite Risings and the personalities of men like Bonnie Prince Charlie.

It might seem strange, given the quality of his work and of his standing in the literary field but what Burns lacks – if that is not too direct a word – is Oliphant's longing for and celebration of the past. He is too political for that. If we take out poems such as *Auld Lang Syne* there is little real sentiment in most of his verse. That doesn't make it poor writing, just the opposite in fact, and in terms of quality poetry *per se* his work is infinitely superior to that of Carolina Oliphant's. But as far as the romantic ideal of Jacobitism is concerned he comes a distinct second.

* * *

The eighteenth century was the great age of satire. In London and in Dublin, two men dominated the world of irony with their poems, books and essays. They were Alexander Pope and Dean Jonathan Swift. Both were active in the first half of the century, dying within a few months of each other in 1744 and 1745 respectively.

Both writers, in their own way, were 'victims' of the post-Glorious Revolution era. With Pope it was because he was a Catholic and chronically disabled by TB of the spine; Swift because his vicious satires had made him an enemy in the shape of the English nobility and Queen Anne herself.

Pope retains the distinction of being the second most quoted writer, behind Shakespeare, in the English language. This is due to his ability to conjure precise and pertinent comments – 'Damned with faint praise' and 'To err is human, to forgive is divine', remain two of his more pertinent efforts. Dean Swift may not be so well quoted but his words remain shockingly powerful – 'A young child, well nursed, is at a year old a most delicious, nourishing and wholesome food.'

Together with writers like John Gay and Henry Fielding, the eighteenth-century satirists were a major force in British literary and social circles, particularly in the years before Culloden and in the immediate aftermath of the defeat. They were the literary opposition to the sentimental view of Jacobitism that, in the wake of Prince Charles' defeat, had become so popular.

Writers like William Makepeace Thackeray and George Borrow were virulent in their condemnation of Jacobite values. Borrow in particular spared no efforts in his attempts to ridicule what he regarded as 'the opposition':

> He linked the rise of sentimental Jacobitism with Catholic Emancipation in England and saw the vogue for Scott and his creations as a Trojan horse for the spread of an aggressive and proselytising Catholics. In his mind Catholicism, Scottishness and Jacobitism were three heads of a single monster.[2]

Henry Fielding was a Whig to the bone and diametrically opposed to what he regarded as backward-looking Jacobites. In books such as *Tom Jones* and *Joseph Andrews* he wrote significantly about his perception of unattractive Tory gentlemen, characters steeped in alcohol, consuming vast excesses of expensive food that ordinary folk could only ever dream about. A playwright and poet as well as one of the country's earliest novelists, Fielding produced some of the strongest anti-Jacobite writing of the era.

He was matched and a little pre-dated by Daniel Defoe. If anything, Defoe was even more virulent than Fielding. The first Poet laureate, John Dryden, was yet another influence on the writers of the time. Although their politics differed, Dryden was a major influence on the development of Henry Fielding. Dryden's refusal to take the oath of allegiance to William and Mary might have lost him the laureateship but it did not lose him his many admirers.

Pro-Jacobite writers started slowly but grew in stature and significance as the eighteenth century drew to an end. In the years after Culloden, the flame of Jacobitism was kept alive, in the main, by poetry and songs where the past was always well-remembered and celebrated.

If there is one word to describe the vast array of sentimental poems from this time, it has to be *lament* where the main impetus is not political or even social but a romantic celebration of all that has gone before.

It requires a degree of maudlin sentiment to write an effective lament but there can be no doubt that maudlin was second nature to the ballad writers of Scotland. As the old saying goes, nobody does maudlin like a Scotsman.

Importantly, these sentimental poems did not directly challenge the Union of England and Scotland, at least not in an overt or obvious way. The writers were careful in taking a more pragmatic and less confrontational approach than the satirists.

They remembered the past, the glory that was to be held and memorised forever in the stories and history of the Jacobite Risings, but the emphasis, with nearly all of the poets and song writers, was one of joint existence. A partnership of equals was their aim. Scotland was not, and never would be, an English colony but as a free-standing country in its own right it had a major role to play.

The sentimentality and romanticism in these productions could hardly have been further away from the satire and sarcasm of Fielding, Pope and the others. Even so, writers like Sir Walter Scott became enormously popular and were soon acknowledging their debt to the satirists, to Jonathan Swift in particular.

And when the Jacobite poets and composers did turn to satire it was not only direct, it was both effective and vicious. *The Riding Mare* is probably one of the most notable ballads of the time although, sadly, the identity of its author remains unknown:

> The Whigs they gave my Auntie draps
> That hastened her away
> And then they took a cursed oath
> And drank it up like whey.
> Then they sent for a bastard race
> Which I may sorely rue
> And for a horse they've got an ass
> And on it set a sow.[3]

The full poem/song satirises two of the pre-Hanoverian monarchs – William III and Queen Anne or Auntie as she is called in the above extract – along with the first of the Hanoverians, King George I.

This verse, however, is not really about the king. It is just one section of a much longer poem, and centres on the Countess of Darlington, mistress to George, who came with him to England when he succeeded to the throne.

Never popular with the people and always a little on the corpulent side, the Jacobites immediately settled on the Countess the nickname 'sow'.

Most Jacobite songs and ballads were neither as satirical nor as clever as *The Riding Mare*. But they were direct and once the writer had decided on his or her theme there was no way of escaping their target:

> Awa, Whigs, awa,
> Awa, Whigs awa,
> Ye're but a pack o' traitor loons,
> Ye'll ne'er do good at a[4]

Most of the Scottish ballads from this time were not published or produced in book form. Some did appear on broadsheets and were sold in the streets and inns but mostly they were just sung in gatherings at places like the local ale house. They were, therefore, mainly anonymous although the audience would have had some idea of the writer's identity.

It was not really until James Hogg's *Jacobite Relics* hit the bookstalls in 1819, followed by a Second Edition two years later, that most of the Ballads appeared in print for the first time. Hogg was a self-taught writer and editor, known as the Ettrick Shepherd, and who became friendly with people like Walter Scott and the poet Allan Cunningham.

Hogg's work in collecting the songs has since been criticised, amongst other things for his re-writing of some of the verses and for including several poems which had nothing whatsoever to do with Jacobitism, but it was still a watershed occasion in the life of the Scottish ballad.

For the first time, the Scots became proud of, as opposed to just enjoying, their literary tradition which was now reaching out beyond the bothies of the Highlands and the public houses or inns of the towns. It was a pride that was to continue for the rest of the century:

> For one poet sprung from the ranks of the English peasantry, Scotland can boast of ten, if not a hundred. Ploughmen, shepherds, gardeners, weavers, tinkers, tailors and even strolling beggars, have enriched the anthology of Scotland with thousands of songs and ballads of no mean merit.[5]

Hogg did try to identify as many of the writers in *Jacobite Relics* as possible but a large number of the poems in the books were doomed to have no attribution. Instead, they saw the first light of day as products from that popular writer who is forever to be known as 'anonymous'.

Looking at the ballads now, many years after they originated, there is a clear definition between verses written by men and verses produced by women. Perhaps the best and most lasting in their appeal are those which bear the clear stamp of female humour and opinion:

> And O, he was a bonnie lad,
> The bravest lad that e'er I saw.
> May ill betide the heathen wight
> That banish'd him and his awa.[6]

At the beginning of the nineteenth-century poets like Allan Cunningham began to make names for themselves, penning lines which have since been taken, altered and made to play a substantial role in modern Scottish songs. Lines such as Cunningham's 'Hame, hame, hame, fain would I be/ Hame, hame, hame to my own countrie' have a resonance that popular singers like Andy Stewart have since made virtually their own.

The Jacobite novel was a little late on the scene but when it did finally arrive it did so with such power and glory that the romanticism of Jacobite Scotland was given a fresh boost. And for that, much of the credit has to go to Sir Walter Scott.

* * *

Sir Walter Scott has been called the founder of historical fiction – and rightly so. Several of his Jacobite novels, *Waverley* for example, set in the 1745 era, and the more renowned *Rob Roy* which has its setting in the years around the 1715 Rising, are examples of first-class fiction bounded by the truth. They remain almost perfect examples of European romanticism.

Born in 1771, Scott – not unlike Alexander Pope – suffered from the disability of a lame leg, the result of a late childhood case of polio. All of his life he walked with a limp and was more than a little conscious of the infirmity. He met Robert Burns when he, Scott, was just fifteen years old and expressed himself impressed. Even so, his greatest early influence was the blind Scottish poet Thomas Blacklock.

Scott began his literary career as an editor and collector of Highland Ballads, spending two decades providing the editorial pages and gathering together the poems to be included in an anthology known as *Minstrelsy*. He remained a collector of broadside ballads all his life.

His own poetic productions began with *The Lay of the Last Minstrel* in 1805, a romance of border chivalry. It was followed by *The Lady of the*

Lake in 1810. Both are narrative poems, what Scott himself would have called novels in poetic form. The latter of the two was phenomenally successful, selling 20,000 copies in its first year alone.

He had begun writing *Waverley* before *The Lay of the Last Minstrel* was published but abandoned it in 1805 after criticism from well-meaning friends and did not return to the partially completed book until 1813. Even renowned and successful authors, it seems, can be affected by adverse criticism!

When *Waverley*, the first of the twenty-seven novels Scott was to write, did finally come out it was after a year of hard scribbling. The book was an immediate success. Perhaps not the easiest of Scott's novels, it remained very popular with the reading public. The rather more accessible *Rob Roy*, centred around the '15 Rising, was the fifth of his prose offerings, a significant part of what is known as the Waverley Series.

He was not always successful in his attempts. Even so, he kept trying. The tinge of romance which makes his writing so different, so expressive, remains to be found in books like *Ivanhoe*, his foray into knightly behaviour and chivalric passions.

While critics were never universally positive in their responses to his style of writing and the idea of 'historical novels,' Scott remained hugely influential with writers as varied as Tolstoy, Dostoevsky, Jane Austen and Emily Bronte. They all praised his books, not only in life but also in their fiction, remarking on his grasp of history and his descriptive skills. In *Middlemarch* George Elliot was to put the following words into the mouth of one of her characters – the second or third reference to Scott in as many chapters of the novel:

> You will not get any writer to beat him, I think – he will not,
> in my opinion, be easily surpassed.[7]

Even American writers such as Nathaniel Hawthorne and Edgar Allen Poe claimed to have written and worked under the direct influence of Walter Scott. While it is all too easy to find metaphors relating to Scott's work, there have been claims that Poe's *The Raven* is really a lament for times gone by. It was certainly written in the style of Scott:

> In there stepped a Raven of the stately days of yore,
> Quoth the Raven, Nevermore.[8]

Scott, as well as working as a Judge Advocate, maintaining his position as a leading member of the Edinburgh Tory circle and writing intense historical novels, continued to compose poetry, producing work like *The Gathering of the Clans* and *Bonnie Dundee*. Romantic and full of longing for the past, the poems clearly indicate his love of Scotland and its history.

Scott was never as direct or as cutting as men like Fielding or Dr Johnson but a piece of satirical verse, found after his death in his collection of broadsides, might possibly show a different side to the man. The poem is unattributed but, having been found amongst his literary leftover scraps, may well belong to Scott. It is harsh, vicious even, in the style of Pope and Swift:

> Ye Whigs are a rebellious crew,
> The plague of this poor nation.
> You give not God nor Caesar due,
> Ye smell of reprobation.[9]

Sir Walter Scott or one of his anonymous collected pieces? It is unlikely that we will ever know the answer to that particular conundrum or question.

* * *

Walter Scott died in 1832, revered and acknowledged as a master of his craft. However, romantic adventure tales from the Jacobite era did not die with him. Other writers soon took up their pens to continue the tradition. The theme was the same, the images and idealism that were continuing and forcing themselves into the Scottish mind-swell of emotion.

Above all, the newer writers seized on the oppression perpetrated by the English in the wake of the '45, moulding the interventions into acts of almost genocidal proportions. Accomplished writers like John Buchan and DK Broster were soon producing quality work, owing much to Scott but focussing on one aspect of historical fact. It was simple enough:

> Deliberate evoking of Scottish nationalist sentimentality about English oppression and the nobility of lost Scottish causes.[10]

One of the earliest exponents and followers of Scott was Robert Louis Stevenson, author of *Treasure Island,* the perennial adventure story of pirates, gold hunting and drama on the high seas. Stevenson was a Jacobite supporter but he had a more pragmatic approach than many of the writers of the time. He could see both sides of the argument and his love of romance came across in the character and adventures of David Balfour, his hero, not in the sentimentality of the Jacobite cause.

Stevenson suffered all his life from ill health. His self-imposed cure was to keep working and before he died in Samoa in 1894, he had travelled all over the world in a desperate attempt to keep active and alive.

Travel as he might, Stevenson's heart was in Scotland and it was in his adventure stories like *Kidnapped*, its sequel *Catriona*, and in *The Wier of Hermiston* that his love of Scotland's history and past came to real fruition.

The Wier of Hermiston, Stevenson's last book, was far deeper than his earlier Scottish-themed tomes, dealing with the breakdown of society which, in turn, leads people into moral ambivalence. The links to the post-Culloden years in Scotland are unmistakeable.

In addition to his novels, Stevenson was also a poet of considerable skill. Significantly, he managed to keep an over-kill of sentiment out of his novels, holding it in readiness for his verse. While not overtly Jacobite in tone, many of his poems have been taken to represent the romantic nature of the movement's passion for life and death, and their longing for a distant, vanished world:

> Under the wide and starry sky
> Dig the grave and let me lie,
> Glad did I live and gladly die
> And I laid me down with a will.[11]

DK Broster, full name Dorothy Kathleen Broster, was a hugely successful novelist writing in the first half of the Twentieth Century. Amongst a mass of other material, she produced a Jacobite trilogy, the first book in the series, called *The Flight of the Heron,* being described as a 'pure masterpiece'.

Henrietta Tayler was also writing mainly in the first half of the twentieth century, her first book appearing in 1914. Born in 1869, she and her brother were confirmed Jacobites and published over thirty full-length works on the subject. Brother and sister worked well together but the real talent lay with the indefatigable Henrietta.

A persistent and highly effective researcher, Hetty as she was known, enlisted as a nurse during the First World War, serving in Belgium, France and Italy. She finished the war as the Matron of a VAD hospital.

Barely five feet tall, Hetty continued researching and working at producing accurate historical views on the Jacobite rebellions, particularly the '15 and the '45. She indexed over 500 volumes of Stuart papers and, using his diary as source material, produced an account of John William O'Sullivan, one of the original Seven Men of Moidart who landed with Bonnie Prince Charlie in 1745 and duly became the Prince's military advisor.[12]

Together with Bishop Robert Forbes who produced the first account of the '45, a volume entitled The Lyon in Mourning, Hetty Tayler was one of the earliest Jacobite historians. Much of what we now know about the two significant Jacobite risings in Britain, the '15 and the '45, is due to her in-depth research and writing.

John Buchan, probably more famous for his thrillers such as *The Thirty-Nine Steps* and *Greenmantle* also produced Jacobite-driven books like *Midwinter* which features Dr Johnson attempting to foil a Jacobite plot at the time of Bonnie Prince Charlie's retreat from Derby.

Buchan's novel came directly out of his Scottish childhood when he was free to roam where he liked across the Scottish hills, allowed to read what he liked and permit his imagination to take him where it may. Nowadays the book is little known but it is brilliantly plotted, convincing many that Buchan's real skill lay not in the genre of action thrillers but in historical romance.

The love of Jacobite ideals and actions did not stop with writers. Catherine Read began her hugely successful career as an artist by painting portraits of local Jacobite families. Hailing from Dundee, she was born in 1723 and was immersed in the Jacobite traditions and history. Her uncle fought in the Jacobite Rising of 1745 and, as a result, the family was forced to flee, first to Paris and then to Rome.

It was in Paris that she began her painting career, becoming a pupil of the Jacobite painter/teacher Robert Strange. She returned to Britain after some years abroad and settled in London where she quickly made a name for herself as a society painter.

Although she painted mainly children and women, it became something of a 'feather in the cap' for Jacobite supporters and friends to own a portrait painted by Catherine Read. When she died in 1778, her significance was such that Catherine was given an epitaph by Tobias Smollett:

> Let candid justice our attention lead
> To the soft crayon of the graceful Catherine Read.[13]

There were so many more writers and artists willing to express themselves for the Hanoverian or the Jacobite cause. In the case of those producing work in the nineteenth and twentieth centuries, they wrote in memory of those causes.

They came from both sides of the political divide and were women and men. However, in the main, women like Dorothy Palmer who wrote letters to her friends and family rather than articles and books had to wait a little longer before achieving equal recognition with the men. When they did turn to pamphlets and the like their work was stunningly stark and yet incredibly beautiful.

Mary Cooper, who partnered Fielding in the writing and production of *The Jacobite's Journal*, Elizabeth Adams and Ann Dodd were just three of the pamphleteers and publishers. They were Hanoverian supporters and vitriolic in their reporting.

The Jacobite movement might have died but the romance of its past, if not its actual chronology, gave impetus to this late flowering of Jacobite thought. For the next two hundred years men and women continued to write poems and songs, novels and short stories, about the Jacobite past. Quality products or second-rate offerings, they remain tributes to a significant part of Scottish history.

Chapter Thirteen

The End of an Era?

Jacobitism did not die on the field of Culloden, there was still hope and enthusiasm in the ranks of Prince Charles Edward's troops. However, even before the defeat there were strong and growing anti-Stuart elements in many parts of Scotland. And those feelings were, in the long run, more powerful, more destructive than any Hanoverian bayonet or cannon ball could ever be.

Much of the disinclination to help the Stuart/Jacobite cause had a distinctly economic basis with trade, particularly overseas trade based on the river Clyde and the suburbs of Glasgow, booming and bringing in large profits for the nation. Why rock the boat, people were beginning to ask, especially now that jobs were plentiful and money readily available?

The long-promised foreign and colonial markets had finally been opened up for Scottish interests and businesses. The wealth that this created was not yet universal but it was getting there and many of the traditional Jacobite supporters, the Macintoshes and the Chisholm's amongst others, decided that it was politic not to take part in the final Rising.[1]

The thorny old chestnut of religion also played a part in the ultimate demise of the Jacobite cause. The Stuarts had already demonstrated their continued adherence to the Catholic faith and the simple fact that James Stuart, the Old Pretender, now lived in Italy, as a guest of the Pope, merely added to the widely held belief that the values or interests of the Stuarts began and ended with the church. Country came only a distant second best.

The Scottish Presbyterian ministers were active in pushing the idea that a return of the Stuarts would lead only to a Papist-supported regime that would do its damndest to destroy Scottish nationhood. Such beliefs simply undermined the foundations of Jacobitism with the result that when Charles was soundly defeated at the Battle of Culloden the strength of emotion that had fuelled the Jacobite cause in the first place was now, at best, somewhat rocky and indecisive.

After defeat and months of running in the heather, Charles headed for home, arriving in France on 10 October 1746. He was determined to return to Britain, as a warrior king rather than a helpless rebel, but it never happened. Hearing of his exploits in Scotland, the people of Paris hailed him as a hero but the French government had grown tired of constant Jacobite wailings and there was no offer of further French military assistance.

Two years later Bonnie Prince Charlie, as he was still known, was expelled from France as part of the Treaty of Aix-la-Chapelle and, thanks to his subsequent refusal to leave the country, was for a short time imprisoned in the Bastille. After that he became something of a nomad, roaming the Continent at will and only returning to Rome after the death of his father in 1766.

It was poor politics on the part of the Prince. His father, James the Old Pretender, had long been recognised by the Papacy as King of England. Prince Charles Edward hoped, in the event of his father's death, for the same recognition but by refusing to come to Rome before his father had actually died, he had shown himself to be grasping and self-centred. All he got from Pope Clement XIII was the empty and pointless title of Count of Albany.

Unable to cope with the gradual demise of Jacobitism, Prince Charles Edward Stuart turned to where he always went in times of trouble – the bottom of the whiskey bottle. He tried to encourage a re-growth of his cause but it was futile. He even offered to convert to Protestantism if that would help his cause.

In fact, Charles' unheralded and surreptitious visit to London in 1750 was intended to mark his conversion. He stayed for several weeks at the home of Jacobite supporter Lady Primrose in her house on Essex Street and was duly inducted into the Protestant faith. But the dream had not died and he was also in England for another, altogether more warlike, reason.

The Elibank Plot, devised and headed by Alexander Murray of Elibank, was an ill-fated attempt to take the Hanoverian royal family hostage and begin a final uprising in favour of the Stuarts. When Charles and the plotters realised that no support was forthcoming either from Prussia or from France the plan fell apart.

Prince Charles headed back to the Continent and the whiskey bottle, screaming about betrayal and cowardice. He also took the opportunity to brutally beat his mistress, Clementina Walkinshaw. From there he descended swiftly into a world of alcohol and physical abuse of the women in his life.

At the end of it all, Charles undoubtedly felt betrayed. His supporting armies who had failed to rout the Redcoats at Culloden; leaders like Lord George Murray who had let him down by turning back at Derby; the French who, in his opinion, had offered much but given little – they had all betrayed him and caused the disaster.

Even his own family had let him down. He had been provided with no training for the role he had to play and there was undoubtedly a very heavy load on his back. It is impossible not to have a degree of sympathy for a man who had never really grown up but was forced to act like a fully-fledged warrior monarch. A degree of sympathy, then, but only a degree.

Charles Edward Stuart's failing relationships with his father and brother reflect not just his opinions on their lack of support but also his ineptitude in making important decisions. His father James, the Old Pretender, had declined into a defeatist. It was a state of mind to which most of the Stuarts were prone to suffer.

Charles, never one to shoulder blame himself, came to believe that his father was a man who had lost all thought of a Stuart return to power. When James gave his blessing to Henry's entry into church 'nobility' it smashed away what few grains of affection that remained. After 1744 Charles Edward Stuart never saw his father again.

Charles' younger brother Henry had shown preference for the church for some time, giving little thought to the Jacobite cause. He would never be forgiven by the grudge-hungry Charles. Neither would Lord George Murray. During the '45 rebellion, Charles had grown to dislike Murray. A few years later dislike had exploded into full-blown hatred. Charles would never forgive him and the pair were never reconciled.

There was, however, just one more chance of a return to Britain and, amazing as it might seem, one last opportunity to reclaim the English crown. It was tenuous and it was perhaps a little foolish but Bonnie Prince Charlie bottled it, big time.

In 1759 an invasion plan involving some 100,000 men was hatched by the French government and Charles Edward was asked to come to Versailles to discuss a possible Jacobite involvement. He arrived drunk and was abusive to the French officials and ministers. Consequently, the French cut the Jacobites out of the invasion plan – which soon fell apart anyway thanks to British naval victories in the Channel – and washed their hands of the Prince.

Charles Edward Stuart died from a stroke on 30 January 1788. He was sixty-seven years old, a poor shrunken shadow of the handsome and elegant young man who had once invaded British shores. Alcohol and disappointment had blighted his life – they were, perhaps, the only things to which he remained true, right to the end of his life.

Much of the blame for Prince Charles' failure to regain the English throne has to rest with him. He was a man of poor judgement, always believing that he was in the right and that his word was the final judgement in any argument. He was inconsistent and fickle, unwilling to take advice and inconsiderate. When you add those qualities to the state of a browbeaten and de-populated Scotland, along with the opinions of its people, it is clear that the defeat of the Jacobite cause was inevitable.

With Prince Charles dead, the mantle of Jacobite Pretender passed to his brother Henry Stuart. And Henry was simply not interested. He and Charles had argued over religion and when Henry was offered and took a Cardinals Hat in 1747 it had proved to be the final straw for Stuart claims to the throne of England.

As Henry was now a formal representative of the religion so hated by the British there was literally no way back for the Stuarts. The situation was further damaged by Henry's alleged homosexuality and, because of his position in the church, the unlikelihood that he would ever father a child. No child equalled no heir and that, of course, meant the continuation of the Hanoverian monarchy. The death knell of Jacobitism could be heard on the other side of the world.

Henry Stuart died in 1807. By then the French Revolution had thrown him into a state of absolute poverty, the new Republic seizing his lands in France and appropriating his various benefices. The Papacy was no longer in a position to help – indeed, Henry had sold the family jewels to help pay fines levied by Napoleon Bonaparte on Pope Pius VI.

At this point George III and the British government stepped in, awarding Henry a pension of £4000 a year. This seeming act of charity was actually nothing of the sort. It was a selfish, Machiavellian act which undermined the charitable gesture by the simple fact that the British government owed a considerable sum of money to the Stuarts, arrears on the jointure of Mary of Modena.

By 1800 the debt was somewhere in the region of three million pounds, a figure which makes George's gesture more than a little disingenuous. And, of course, the balance was never paid. £4000 was all the Stuarts ever received.

Money was one thing, the sad state of the lower-class Jacobite supporters was another thing altogether. Many of them paid for their Jacobite support with their lives or their sanity and it was all too easy to sway wildly between a pro-Jacobite stance and an anti-one.

Isabel Campbell is now a little-known character. She nursed her husband Robert, a tailor who had been 'pressed' into service with Prince Charles' army, for seven long weeks before he died from dysentery. No time to grieve, she was then sent to assist the surgeon in Carlisle Castle, tending to wounded Jacobites. She had no choice in the matter and certainly received no wages for her work.

Despite her clear Jacobite connections, the stresses and pressures on Isabel must have been enormous as, once the rebellion was over, she quickly turned King's Evidence. Her evidence in court, sometimes under direct questioning, sometimes as voluntary statements, sent many Jacobite soldiers to their deaths or to jail.

Being a turncoat and changing sides was not uncommon. In the wake of Culloden, many men and women chose to betray former comrades in order to save their own lives. Anne Hickson and her husband John were two, Sarah Holland another. Sarah pointed the finger at a Jacobite soldier who had lodged with her as Prince Charles' army marched south to Derby and then refreshed her memory by going back to her house to collect possessions he had left behind.

Turning King's Evidence might have been unpalatable to most Jacobites but it undoubtedly saved the lives of many rebel women. They received free pardons from the State and were allowed to return home. When there were children to consider that was nothing to be sniffed at.

* * *

Jacobitism might be dead but the later Hanoverians along with their Victorian counterparts eagerly seized on Scottish culture and history, purloining them for their own ends. It began as a freak of fashion, a hobby that was started by George IV, but soon morphed into a way of life, a cult that was both acceptable to those in control of the country and a viable alternative to the now-distant threat of Jacobitism.

Led by Queen Victoria herself, the wearing of tartan became almost *de rigour* in some quarters, tartan trews, kilts and shawls being just the tip of the iceberg. Affiliation and the attribution of specific tartans to various Scottish clans was a largely fictional affectation but it became something of a cult practice in Victorian England.

Scottish reels and other dances, Scottish folk music and ballads, the novels of men like Sir Walter Scott became, under the 'benign' rule of Victoria, a significant part of British society, particularly for the upper classes. Nobles and wealthy individuals were soon combing their family lineage in an effort to find Scottish ancestors. If they couldn't find any, they invented them! And the royal family, German to the core, were no different.

Royal castles such as Balmoral and Holyrood Palace, along with dozens of other smaller houses and lodges, provided palatial residences for royalty when they felt inclined to take in the Scottish atmosphere. The men might shoot on the grouse moors but for the women, it was a time of relaxation, of carriage rides and the luxury of reading books from the pen of Sir Walter Scott, Robert Louis Stevenson and others. Individuals like John Brown, ex-gillie for Prince Albert, friend and servant to the Queen, were always on hand to guide and protect his royal charges.

It was a strange turn of attitude from the people who had caused the Jacobite demise but by then, a hundred or so years after Culloden, there was no danger of further insurrection. It was, in the eyes of most Victorians, a harmless holiday pastime in a land populated by peaceful, friendly allies.

Indeed, rather than out-and-out rebels, the Scots had now become significant players in the success of the British Empire. As soldiers of the Queen, as statesmen, officials and administrators they had helped in major events like the conquest of the Indian sub-continent and in extending the long arm of British interests into many different parts of the world. By the middle years of the nineteenth century, Jacobitism was, frankly, irrelevant.

Jacobite estates and houses confiscated by the government after 1745 were finally restored to the rightful owners in 1784, four years before the death of Bonnie Prince Charlie. At the same time, the Episcopalian church declined to offer prayers for the exiled Stuarts, something the church had been doing since 1688. It was a significant moment, the final death throes of a movement which had for too long continued to survive on a diet of emotionally charged ballads and poetry.

Where the last remnants of Jacobitism did survive, as in Ireland, they did so as examples of republicanism rather than support for a long-gone monarchy. The aim was no longer to restore a monarchical line but to undermine and destroy rule by a distant and alien governing clique.

It was a sad end for Jacobitism. The Battle of Culloden alone had produced a huge Jacobite death toll of around 2000 along with nearly 4000 Scottish, English and French soldiers being imprisoned once the after-battle massacres had finished.

Of those 4000, men and women who were flung without much thought into jails across the country, 120 were hanged, 936 transported and over 600 died in prison. If that seems to be an over-estimate it is worth remembering the story of just one prison ship which sailed for London soon after the Battle of Culloden. Of 157 prisoners on board, only 49 were alive when the ship docked at Tilbury.

The prison ships were really coffin ships, conditions and treatment of the captives being deliberately horrendous. No distinction was drawn between men and women captives and regular whippings and deprivation of food and water were common occurrences. Jacobite doctors were even denied their equipment, bags of which were usually thrown overboard, so that they could not treat sick or injured comrades.

Such sacrifices as those endured by the Jacobite prisoners were the bedrock of the various risings. Nobody had ever wanted to make such sacrifices but everyone knew they were possible, if not likely, and when the leaders proved inadequate and insubstantial the wonder is that the movement survived as long as it did.

※ ※ ※

Much has been written about the various Jacobite risings, the '45 more than any of the others. And it all began with an amazing factual account of that final rebellion, entitled *The Lyon in Mourning*, written by Robert Forbes, Bishop of Ross and Caithness.

A Jacobite by inclination and upbringing, Forbes had joined the Episcopalian clergy in 1708. He rose steadily through the ranks until in

The End of an Era?

1762 he was appointed Bishop of Ross and Caithness. He had joined the Jacobite forces during the rising of 1745 but was arrested before any of the serious conflicts and imprisoned for over twelve months in Stirling and Edinburgh Castles.

Released in May 1746, Forbes immediately began to gather together accurate and descriptive eye-witness accounts of the rebellion. With painstaking accuracy and skill, he covered the road to Culloden, the battle itself and its after effects, interviewing participants, taking first-hand testimonies and copying letters from a whole range of interested parties.

Over a frantically active and intense five-year period Robert Forbes compiled eight volumes of memories and recollections, each of 200 pages. Two more volumes followed but the final one lay unfinished because of his death in November 1775.

Even now, the accounts are still vivid and Forbes' handling of the material is immaculate. One of his chief informants was Ned Burke, a Jacobite cavalryman who gave a scintillating account of how he came across the Prince as the royal leader fled the field of battle.

Ned Burke also named Flora MacDonald and described her part in the affair, the first time that the young woman who helped Bonnie Prince Charlie to escape had ever been named. It is hard to know whether or not that identification did Flora good or harm but it was a sound historical fact that needed to be recorded.

Over the years there have been dozens of accounts, factual and fictional, of the various risings but *The Lyon in Mourning* is the original and, being based on personal, first-hand accounts, is probably one of the best. It was later reworked by Henry Paton and published by the Scottish Historical Society in 1895.[2]

Albeit from a Jacobite perception, Forbes' book was accurate and condemnatory of many Hanoverian practices, particularly those of Butcher Cumberland in the aftermath of the final battle. It, therefore, did nothing to ease the sense of injustice that still lingered in some quarters.

With all likelihood of a Stuart/Jacobite victory now gone, the romantic sentimentality of the Jacobite ballads from this time came to focus on the legend, myth and unfulfilled dream provided by Bonnie Prince Charlie.

They still centred on the promises made by the Stuarts, but there were also examples of a harder edge in some of the poetry and a bitter resentment can still be found. Most of the ballads were, as ever, anonymous but some came from rather unexpected sources.

Thomas Babington Macauley, the 1st Baron Macauley, was an historian of note although his work has rather gone out of fashion these days. A pillar of Georgian society, he was also a poet, best known for his epic poem 'Horatius', about the Roman Empire. He also produced this piece, decidedly English and decidedly Jacobite. It is an heroic stance, quite what his real feelings might have been remains unclear:

> To my true king I offer'd free from strain
> Courage and faith, vain faith, and courage vain.
> For him I threw lands honours, wealth, away
> And one dear hope that was more prized than they.
> For him I languished in a foreign clime,
> Grey-hair'd with sorrow in my manhood's prime.
> O thou, whom chance leads to this nameless stone,
> From this proud country which was once mine own.
> By these white cliffs I never more must see
> By that dear language which I spoke like thee.
> Forget all feuds, and shed one English tear
> O'er English dust. A broken heart lies here.[3]

Even here, in Macauley's unexpected and clearly romanticised poem, it is impossible to escape the sentiment and sense of longing, contrived as it may be, which dominated much poetic thinking at this time. We come back, once again, to the idea of lamenting the past.

The end of the Jacobite era left behind vanished hopes and old worn-out dreams of what might have been. Sentimental ballads and stories about Scottish heroes like Rob Roy, Bonnie Prince Charlie, Flora MacDonald, Jenny Cameron and the others make wonderful and attractive reading. But they were not real then and remain unreal even now. Defeat and years of disdain, of being regarded as a nation and a people who were no-hopers or also-rans, that was real.

Not real is a description that can be applied to two female imposters who surfaced in the wake of the Battle of Culloden, both of them claiming to be the famous Jenny Cameron. The real Jenny was a Jacobite hero who, at the time, achieved almost the same level of fame as Flora MacDonald.

The End of an Era?

The Hanoverian government sought to blacken Jenny's name by the use of tall tales about her propensity for wearing men's clothes and her supposed promiscuity and sexual appetite. Booklets and leaflets were used to bolster the rumours but managed only to increase her popularity and make her a fascinating figure in Jacobite folk lore.

The first imposter was actually a milliner from Edinburgh who travelled to Stirling to help an injured relative. The Duke of Cumberland was convinced she was the real Jenny Cameron and had her imprisoned in Edinburgh Castle where she stayed for nearly a year.

During this time a pamphlet was published claiming that the imposter was actually the mistress of Prince Charles. When she was finally released from custody and re-opened her Edinburgh milliners shop, business was, to say the least, booming. Whatever denials were made, most of the customers were still convinced that she had been the Prince's concubine.[4]

The second imposter did not fare quite so well. Real name Sarah Waugh, at various times and in various towns she claimed to be several different people, Jenny Cameron amongst them.

Jenny Cameron was perhaps her most infamous false disguise but she also told people that she was the wife of a Captain Drummond who had been killed at Culloden. She had fought alongside him, Sarah claimed, and received a wound to the face, thus neatly explaining away the long, cruel cut across her cheek.

Sarah wandered from town to town in the north of England, telling her different stories and receiving alms or help from those she could convince of her imagined identity. For a short while, she was a renowned figure, her Jenny Cameron persona being particularly successful.

The truth, of course, was very different. Sarah was clearly mentally unstable and had, it seemed, spent some time in the Bedlam asylum in London.

After being apprehended in Newcastle she was interrogated when 'it was discovered, after enquiries, that she had been "no more than a basket wench".' She had delivered meat, fruit and other commodities to the homes of the wealthy and kept what was described as 'the very worst of company'.[5]

***

It still remains very easy to allot or allocate blame for the failure of the various Jacobite risings, just as it was back in the eighteenth century.

Nobody doubted the fighting qualities of the Highlanders who had battled on when outnumbered and faced with superior weapons and equipment. The leaders of the risings, however – well, that was a different matter altogether.

If the men at the top of the Jacobite tree – James II, James III or the Old Pretender, and Bonnie Prince Charlie – had been more adept, driven more by concerns about the people and less by their religion and status as monarchs of the Stuart dynasty then perhaps the outcome of the various risings might have been different. Perhaps.

Apart, perhaps, from James II, none of them was a particularly able leader. The most charismatic of them was Charles Edward Stuart, the Bonnie Prince Charlie of legend and folk lore.

Charismatic Charles may have been but he was, like his father and grandfather before him, also a shallow man, filled with insecurities and contradictions of character. He had a propensity to change his affiliations or friendship at the drop of a hat. His relationship with Lord George Murray is a classic example with the general dropping out of favour as soon as he disagreed with the Prince over tactics at the Battle of Prestonpans.

Bonnie Prince Charlie's greatest failure as a man and a leader, however, was in not recognising that following the defeat at Culloden the Jacobite cause was finished. Whatever might be said of his father, the Old Pretender, James III certainly knew his limitations. He knew when to fight, knew when to retire – and when to stay at home and let younger men take up arms on his behalf.

The anger and bitterness Prince Charles displayed, before, during and after Culloden, his regrets and disappointments, grew from this inability to see what so many others – his father and brother included – could understand and recognise so easily. And in the end, it was that failure to see reality which destroyed him.

Chapter Fourteen

Final Thought

No matter where you stand politically, socially and historically, it is almost impossible to view the Jacobite era – and it is an era, the likes of which we may never see again - without the powerful shades of sentimental romanticism creeping into the picture.

Many historians and writers see the various Jacobite risings as inconsequential and as easily dealt with as a fly settling on a cow's rump. Regardless of those opinions and however you look at the events which followed James II's flight in 1688, that view has to be challenged.

The hundred-year period of riot and rebellion which symbolises the Jacobite rebellions has all the hallmarks of great and noble adventure. It contains moments of death, glory and disaster; it has all the traits and tropes of what was to be, ultimately, a tragic failure; it owns moments of great courage along with many instances of cowardice, cruelty and fear. It has produced fascinating literature, settled distinctive images and sayings onto our culture, and created a unique dress code.

The Jacobite era remains one of the most powerful and dramatic periods in British history. It has long held a vital place in the memory of most children. There cannot be many British people, regardless of their precise nationality – English, Scottish, Welsh or Irish – who haven't sung *The Skye Boat Song* or viewed pictures of a defiant Flora MacDonald braving the storm in the tiny boat with Prince Charles while Redcoat soldiers stand, afraid to follow, on the shore.

Even the name of Bonnie Prince Charlie is renowned, along with the toast to *The King Across the Water* and the terms Old and Young Pretender. They are, quite simply, fixed in our vocabulary and culture.

The story of exiled King James' defeat at the Battle of the Boyne has gone down as a seminal moment in English and Irish history, commemorated every summer by Irish Protestants. And, of course, the scuffles and the fighting also remain.

The siege of Derry is equally well remembered while the life and death of Scotland's Bonnie Dundee have been commemorated in many poems and songs. The famous Highland Ballads, lamenting the going of Bonnie Prince Charlie and others, are still performed and sung by men and women who might have never crossed the Scottish border in their lives.

Perhaps, then, Jacobitism remains so potent a memory because we have been brain washed by the stories, by the events and by the people involved. We continue to be enthralled by the Jacobite legends that are as riveting as those of King Arthur, Alfred the Great and the defeat of the Spanish Armada.

Trying to take an objective view of the Jacobite era is damned difficult. Inevitably, half-forgotten, half-remembered dreams and visions from the past will flood your senses when you read about things like the flight of Bonnie Prince Charlie and the heroism of Flora MacDonald. Arguably the era has become the preserve of the story teller rather than the historian.

If that is right, then perhaps it is how it should be. Dry, dusty facts can be off-putting. Romantic stories catch the imagination and enable the people of the present to better understand the people of the past.

Arguably, that is the best way to learn. That is if we want to ensure that mistakes made hundreds of years ago are not repeated over and over again. As Rudyard Kipling once declared 'If history were to be taught through the medium of stories we would all remember it much better and not keep making the same mistakes.'

And yet, romance and sentiment are all very well but they are hardly the stuff from which strong monarchies and empires are built. They come after the event, at the end of an era, celebrating or lamenting it but hardly creating it.

In part, Jacobitism failed because the romance and sentiment grew to be more powerful than the original aims of the movement. The events of the sixty or so years between 1688 and 1746 were momentous but, at the end of the day, they were fragile in their makeup and grounded in nothing more than hopes and ambitions.

Any regime or power driven solely by dreams is, ultimately, bound to fail. The examples are obvious – the Greek city states of the Ancient World, the Confederacy during the American Civil War, even the Jacobite cause itself. Viewed, now, in hindsight, defeat and retribution were always waiting in the wings for the Jacobite movement to implode and destroy itself:

> Jacobitism survived for as long as it did because various Continental powers encouraged and sustained it. Jacobitism was obviously useful as a latent threat with which to exert pressure on the Whig regime in Britain.[1]

There is little more to be said. The Stuart dynasty effectively died after James fled the country in what we still refer to as the Glorious Revolution of 1688. The power and influence of the Stuart monarchy withered and declined at that point along with the persona of James II.

What we are left with now are a clutch of magnificent stories, a batch of startling heroes and villains and a nod of approval in the direction of true democracy and peace. We can ask for nothing more.

Notes

Chapter One – An Introductory Prologue

1. Kenyon, JP, 'Stuart England,' p. 209
2. Devine, TM, 'The Scottish Nation,' p.36
3. Nairne, Margaret, et al, 'A Bundle of Jacobite Letters,' Various writers
4. https://enwikipedia.org.wiki/Jacobitism
5. Ibid

Chapter Two – A Resignation and a Revolution

1. Devine, p. 82
2. Pepys, Samuel, 'Diary, September 1666'
3. Quoted in Tinniswood, Alan, 'By Permission of Heaven'
4. Devine, p. 32
5. Ibid, p. 32

Chapter Three – Mary of Modena and Grizzel Mhor Grant, Jacobite Heroines

1. https://www.bing.com/Mary-of-Modena
2. Kenyon, p. 209
3. Anon, 'Antiquarian Notes,' Chapter 27
4. Ibid, Chapter 17
5. Devine, Page XXi
6. Quoted in www.glencoe.massacre
7. Hufton, Olwen, 'The Prospect Before Her,' p. 463
8. Ibid, p. 463
9. McLynn, Frank, 'The Jacobites', p. 156
10. Ibid, p. 55

Chapter Four – Yet More Chances

1. Devine, Ibid, p. 34
2. Scott, Sir Walter, 'Rob Roy,' p. 55

Chapter Five – The '15 Rising: Jacobite Women Flex Their Muscles

1. McLynn, Ibid, p. 95
2. McLynn, Ibid, p. 99
3. Quoted on www.//find-my-past.co.uk
4. Ibid
5. www://find-my-past/history/Jacobite-women
6. Anon/Various, 'Memoirs of the Jacobites,' p. 38
7. Ibid, p. 41
8. Quoted in Maggie Craig, 'Damn' Rebel Bitches,' p. 182
9. Fielding, Henry, 'The Jacobite Journal' 1745 (National Newspaper Library)
10. http://www.historyhid.com
11. Dalton, Isaac, 'The Shift Shifted,' 16-94, 18 August 1716

Chapter Six - Try, Try, Try Again – and an Unexpected Jacobite Hero

1. www://en.wikipedia.org/Maria-Clementina-Sobienska
2. Roberts, Doreen 'Introduction' to reprint of 'Tom Jones,' 1999
3. Maggie Craig, Ibid, p. 63
4. Szechi, Daniel, 'The Jacobites,' p. 5
5. Ibid, pp. 24-25
6. Quoted in https://www.pascalbonefont.com
7. Timbs, John, 'Club Life of London,' Vol 1
8. Maggie Craig, Ibid, p. 37
9. https://Sankey, Margaret/www.routledge.com/Jacobite-Prisons-of-the-1715-Rebellion
10. Ibid
11. www://electricsotland.com/history/American/scots-prisons
12. https://www.bartlely.com/essay/Jacobite/women

Chapter Seven – Jacobite Calling Cards

1. Szechi, Daniel, Ibid, p. 87
2. https://nationalarchives.gov.uk/education
3. https://en.wikipedia.org.wiki/The-Bonnie-Bankso'-Loch-Lomond

4. Burns, Robert, 'The Complete Poems'
5. https://en.wikipedia.org/wiki/The-Wee-Germain-Lairdie
6. MacDiarmid, Hugh, 'Introduction; The Golden Treasury of Scottish Poetry,' Page XI
7. https://en.wikipedia.org.wiki/history-of-the -world
8. Ibid
9. www://thehistoryjar.com/Jacobites
10. Murphy, Sean, 'Irish Jacobites and Freemasons,' article in 'Eighteenth Century Ireland,' pp. 75-82
11. Maggie Craig, Ibid, pp. 14-15
12. Ibid, p. 18
13. Anon, 'This is Not the End,' article by Vanessa Iacocca in 'Discovery'

Chapter Eight – The Coming of the Prince and the Lady of Lude

1. Szechi, Daniel, Ibid, p. 96
2. Letter in www.bartlely.com
3. www.charlotte-robertson.com
4. www.bing.search.Charlotte.Robertson

Chapter Nine – Culloden and the Women of the Battlefield

1. Szechi, Daniel, Ibid, p. 100
2. www.wikipedia.org
3. Affairs of Scotland, Page 336-41, quoted in 'The Jacobites,' Szechi, p. 147
4. Szechi, Daniel, Ibid, pp. 101-102
5. McLynn, Frank 'The Jacobites,' Ibid, p. 117
6. Ibid, p. 118
7. www.scotsman.com/lost-children-1745
8. www.bellacaledonian.org.uk
9. Ibid
10. www.bellacaledonian.org.uk/Anne/Mckay
11. Maggie Craig, Ibid, p. 91
12. Ibid, p. 92

Chapter Ten – Jacobite Women, Heroes of the '45

1. www.en.wikipedia.org/wiki/Jean-Cameron
2. www.bellacaledonian.org.uk
3. https://www.findmypast.co.uk

Notes

4. Quoted in https://www.historyscotland.com/history/spotlight-jacobites-lady-of-swords
5. Boswell, James, 'Journal of a Tour to the Hebrides,' p. 132
6. Johnson, Dr Samuel, 'Journey to the Western Islands of Scotland,' p. 137
7. Maggie Craig, Ibid, pp. 112-113
8. Ibid, p. 115
9. Johnson, Dr Samuel, on Memorial Plaque for Flora MacDonald in Kilmuir Cemetery

Chapter Eleven – The Clearances and More

1. Scott, Sir Walter 'Rob Roy,' p. 506
2. McLynn, Frank Ibid, p. 127
3. Ibid, p. 127
4. Ibid, p. 154
5. Quoted on www://facebook
6. www://scotsman.com

Chapter Twelve – Literary Jacobite Women and Men

1. www://wikipedia.org/wiki/Carolina-Nairne
2. McLynn, Frank, Ibid, p. 213
3. 'The Riding Mare,' Traditional Jacobite Song in 'The Jacobite Relics' by James Hogg, p. 50
4. Anon, 'Awa Whigs, Awa,' Jacobite song in 'The Jacobite Relics,' p. 62
5. McKay, Charles, Introduction 'Jacobite Songs and Ballads,' p. 1
6. Ibid
7. Elliot, George, 'Middlemarch,' p. 347
8. Poe, Edgar Allen, 'The Raven,' p. 12
9. Hogg, James (editor), 'The Jacobite Relics,' p. 69
10. MacDonald, Kate, https://www.handheldpress.co.uk
11. Stevenson, Robert Louis, 'Requiem,' from 'Collected Poems,' Edinburgh University Press, Edinburgh, 2003
12. Smollett, Tobias, quoted on www://en.wikipedia.org/wiki/Catherine-Read

Chapter Thirteen – The End of an Era

1. Devine, TM, 'The Scottish Nation,' p. 48
2. Discovery Magazine, 2009

3. Macauley, Thomas Babington Macauley, 'Epitaph on a Jacobite' from 'The Poems of Thomas Babington Macauley'
4. Major, Joanne and Murden, Sarah 'All Things Georgian,' pp. 38-43
5. Ibid, p. 42

Chapter Fourteen - Final Thought

1. Szechi, Daniel, Ibid, p. 138

Bibliography

Primary Sources

Anon 'Antiquarian Jacobite Notes,' genealogical and social interest, Inverness, parish by parish
Anon, 'Memoirs of the Jacobites'
Anon 'Bundle of Jacobite Letters' including several from Margaret Nairne, Inverness
Anon 'The Scottish Minstrel,' six volumes 1821 to 1824
Dalton, Isaac 'The Shift Shifted,' newspaper/magazine, 1716
Hogg, James (AKA The Ettrick Shepherd), 'The Jacobite Relics' Edinburgh University Press – originally published 1819, this edition 2003
Letter, George Miller to Everard Faulkner, 12 July 1746, RA CP/Main Box 17/240
Timbs, John 'Club Life of London,' Vol 1, 1866
(NB Many of the above are now available online. Several, if not all, of the papers/magazines can also be found in the National Newspaper Archive, Hendon)

Books/Secondary Sources

Burns, Robert, 'Collected Poems' Wordsworth Poetry Library, London
Craig, Maggie, 'Damn Rebel Bitches,' Mainstream Publishing, Edinburgh, 1997
Devine, TM 'The Scottish Nation,' Penguin, London, 1999
Elliot, George, 'Middlemarch,' Penguin, London, 1872, new edition 2001

Fielding, Henry, 'Tom Jones,' Wordsworth Classics, London, 1999 – first published 1746, new edition published 1999

Flower, Margaret & Desmond 'Cassell's Anthology of English Poetry,' Cassell, London, undated

Hufton, Olwen 'The Prospect Before Her,' Harper Collins, London, 1995

Kenyon, JP 'Stuart England,' Penguin, London, 1978

Macauley, Thomas Babington 'The Collected Poems,' Kessinger Press, London

MacDiarmid, Hugh (editor) 'Golden Treasury of Scottish Poetry,' Macmillan, London, 1946

McKay, Charles (editor) 'Jacobite Songs and Ballads,' Griffin and Co, Edinburgh, 1829

Major, Joanne & Murden, Sarah 'All Things Georgian,' Pen & Sword, Barnsley, 2019

McLynn, Frank 'The Jacobites,' Routledge & Kegan Paul, London, 1985

Poe, Edgar Allen 'The Raven,' Sig Publishing, London, 2020

Rogers, Pat (editor) 'Johnson and Boswell in Scotland,' Yale, New Haven, 1993 – reprinting two books on tours through Scotland by Johnson and Boswell

Scott, Sir Walter 'Rob Roy,' Penguin, London, 1995, first published 1817

_____ 'Waverley,' Penguin, London, 2013, first published 1825

Smollett, Tobias 'The Tears of Scotland,' London, 1746

Stephenson, Robert Louis 'Kidnapped,' first Published in 'Young Folk Magazine,'1886, 'Collected Poems,' Edinburgh University Press, 2003

Szechi, Daniel 'The Jacobites,' Manchester University Press, Manchester, 1994

Tinniswood, Adrian 'Permission of Heaven: The Great Fire of London," Cape, London, 2003

Williams, EN 'A Documentary History of England,' Penguin, London, 1965

Magazines/Newspapers

BBC History Magazine – all issues for 2022-2023

Bibliography

Discovery Magazine, published by the National Library of Scotland – various issues from Spring 2006
Eighteenth Century Ireland, Vol 9, January 1994
Scotsman, The (daily paper) – various issues, 2022-2023

Websites/pages

https://britannica.com
https://www.bing.com/Mary-of-Modena
https://en.wikipedia.org/wikki/Catherine-Read
https://thehistoryjar.com/jacobite-symbols
https://en.wikipedia.org/wiki/carolina-nairne
https://www.bartlely.com/Jacobite/women
https://bellacaledonia.org.uk
https://www.electricscotland.com
www.scotsman.com.lost-children-1745
https://blog-gale-com/scottish-romanticism-and-the-jacobites
https://nationalarchives.gov.uk/education
https://www.find-my-past/history/Jacobite-women